CHRONICLES OF WHITEFISH BAY WISCONSIN

On the cover: This photograph, taken in 1918 on the steps of Fleetwood Grade School in Whitefish Bay, shows students from grades five through eight with their instructors standing behind. Notice the bicycle propped against the porch (photo right). This may be one of the last photographs taken at the school before it was destroyed by fire later that year. *Whitefish Bay Historical Society.*

CHRONICLES OF

WHITEFISH BAY WISCONSIN

Edited by THOMAS H. FEHRING

Published by The History Press
Charleston, SC 29403
www.historypress.net

First published 2013

ISBN 978.1.5402.2237.4

Library of Congress CIP data applied for.

Notice: The information in this book is true and complete to the best of our knowledge. It is offered without guarantee on the part of the author or The History Press. The author and The History Press disclaim all liability in connection with the use of this book.

Published with the assistance of the Whitefish Bay Historical Society and the Whitefish Bay Historic Preservation Commission.
Visit us on the internet at: http://wfbhistoricalsociety.webs.com

CONTENTS

Contents

ACKNOWLEDGEMENTS

I would like to acknowledge and thank the following for their helpful assistance:

- The Whitefish Bay Historical Society for providing use of its historic files along with historic photographs of the village.
- The members of the Whitefish Bay Historic Preservation Commission for providing support and encouragement toward this endeavor.
- The librarians at the Whitefish Bay library for their frequent and helpful assistance.
- Dr. Elizabeth Fulmer and her extended family, who graciously allowed publication of articles on Whitefish Bay written by her mother, Gloria Rockwood Houghton, and to Deborah Houghton Schmidt for providing family photographs to help illustrate the stories.
- Robert C. Johnson, who wrote the tragic story about his grandparents Ray and Ora Belle Tompkins.
- My wife, Suzan, for putting up with the many hours I spent working on this project, and my daughter, Alicia, for reviewing the text and catching many of my mistakes.

Unless otherwise noted, stories and images appear courtesy of the Whitefish Bay Historical Society and the Whitefish Bay Library. They jointly maintain the village's Historical Collection, which includes the Mimi Bird Files—an invaluable source of village history. Most images were scanned from the Historical Collection or obtained directly from the WFB Historical Society's files.

Finally, this work could not have been prepared without the previous extensive research of members of the WFB Historical Society, past and present, upon which I relied heavily—most notably, the work of Mimi Bird and Lewis Herzog—to whom the village is indebted.

INTRODUCTION

This is a history of Whitefish Bay, Wisconsin, told largely through the letters and recollections of early residents of the village.

When Whitefish Bay formed a historic preservation commission in 2005, I was fortunate to be selected as one of its charter commissioners. I gravitated into the research historian role—one that was needed to document the historic homes and other buildings within the community. This was the start of my exploration of the history of the area. I found that there are stories behind literally every house within the village.

I authored a book in 2010 consisting largely of images of Whitefish Bay, using some of the many photographs in the village's historical collection. After publication, several early residents of the village wrote letters about how the book triggered memories of their years in the community. I began accumulating these letters with the thought that they would be of interest to others.

In my research, I became aware of the information that was available in the Mimi Bird files, also known as the Whitefish Bay Historical Collection. As part of her research, Mimi had painstakingly accumulated numerous letters about the history of the village and had also assembled a number of oral histories of early residents. Additionally, the Whitefish Bay Historical Society had independently collected a number of interesting stories.

As a result of the availability of all of these stories, this book has been largely written by others, making my task relatively easy. I hope that it provides current residents with a sense of what it was like to live in the

A Whitefish Bay student outing to Fox Point for a class picnic. The students are not known, nor is the date of the outing, but they appear to be having a good time. *Whitefish Bay Historical Society.*

community of Whitefish Bay during its formative years. And for others, it should provide insights into life in Wisconsin in the nineteenth and twentieth centuries.

My personal history in Whitefish Bay extends back to only 1973. Most of the history contained in these pages predates that year by decades. While I have attempted to be thorough in my research and have relied on the distinguished work of former village historians, errors may have occurred. If I have misinterpreted some of the history, I apologize.

I enjoyed gathering these stories of the village. I have made some minor edits to the original text in some stories, mainly to conform to current punctuation styles and to trim some of the missives down to a reasonable size. I added some illustrations to help bring the stories to life.

The most difficult task in publishing this book involved the final selections. Inevitably, many interesting stories had to be excluded, and space did not permit several stories to be fully told. Perhaps at some point there will be enough material for another volume.

I hope you enjoy this trip through our past.

Chapter 1

GLIMPSES INTO OUR VILLAGE'S PAST

BY LEWIS W. HERZOG, TEXT OF A SPEECH GIVEN IN 1963

Lewis Herzog was an active member of the Whitefish Bay Historical Society for many years. During his tenure, he researched the village's early history. I thought it would be a good starting point for this book.

I am not one of the old-timers, although I may sound like one as the result of frequent conversations I have had with early settlers here. My interest in Whitefish Bay goes back only a matter of twenty years, when my wife and I fell in love with the beautiful silver beech trees on the south side of Fleetwood Place across from the present library building. We bought the lot and, in 1940, built our home there. I was interested in the many carvings of initials, entwined hearts, etc., on the smooth bark of my trees and asked my friend, the late Ernie Dunlap, how they got there. He said, "The school kids"; I said, "What school?" So he took me across the street and showed me the old basement walls of what he said was the original school that was responsible for the incorporation of our village in 1892, just seventy-one years ago.

To answer the "How and Why," I began to do a little research work, which has continued to this day; someday I hope to write a complete definitive history. Meanwhile, I have had several stories published and will quote from some of them as I go along.

Much of my information has come from the perusal of abstracts of title, usually considered dry legal documents but really a gold mine of data on landownership, debts, boom times and depressions and often enlivened with intensely interesting personal items as well.

Fleetwood School in 1893, one year after the Village of Whitefish Bay was incorporated. *Whitefish Bay Historical Society.*

Take the Whitefish Bay Women's Club property for example. It was part of an eighty-acre tract sold by the U.S. government at the Land Office in Green Bay in September 1835 to one Garret V. Denniston for $1.25 per acre. I dare say that the Whitefish Bay Women's Club paid slightly more for it. The tract then extended from what is now Idlewild Avenue on the east to Santa Monica Boulevard on the west and from Silver Spring on the north to

Henry Clay on the south. Denniston was probably a land speculator, for he soon sold the property to a John Arndt, who sold it in turn to George Boyd in 1845. In 1850, Catherine Hamilton bought the eighty acres. Stability came to the tract two years later, when an English-born farmer, John Swain, began to farm the land. In 1864, his son, William, took over. In 1874 a small piece in the northeast corner was sold to the old Milwaukee, Lake Shore and Western Railroad for their right of way. It is interesting to note that this right of way followed the old Sauk Indian trail, and no wonder, for the Indians were no more interested in climbing grades than were the railroad engineers. In 1880, John Burke and Richard Mann bought the farm as an investment, but their plans for profit did not pay off until many years later, despite the fact that subdivision of surrounding land began as early as 1887.

For a time, a Polish-born farmer named Krych operated a dairy farm and after that the land lay fallow until 1925, when the Lake Crest Development Co. acquired the property, which at long last was subdivided in 1927. The only vestiges of the farm that remain are the apple trees in the old orchard on the east side of Hollywood Avenue a short distance south of Silver Spring.

But what about the birth of the village? Apparently, it was conceived in the mind of George A. Rogers, who published a weekly newspaper, the *Whitefish Bay Pioneer*, and who, from the first issue on January 16, 1882, beat the editorial drums for a village charter so that a new school district could be set up. The area that is now Whitefish Bay was once part of the Town of Milwaukee, which then had two schools—the Lindwerm School on the Port Road, north of Hampton, and the Greentree School, also on the old Port Road, a short distance south of the Greentree Road. The first is gone, but you can still see the second building as part of the School Tavern. Notice this the next time you drive by. You can tell it by the tall, old-fashioned windows, characteristic of the schoolhouses of that period. The earlier settlers like the Markerts, Everts, Rabes and Grams did not object too much to having their children walk several miles to school, but as the population grew in this area, the parents petitioned the Town Board for a new school closer to home—but to no avail. Therefore, when Rogers sounded the call for action, he got enthusiastic support. Several mass meetings resulted in a decision to incorporate a village.

The first step was to prove that the 300 people required by state law lived within the limits of the proposed village. Henry Scheife was given the job of making the official census. He told me that he was short of the necessary 300 and had to go a bit farther south to pick up what he needed—hence the jog in the southern boundary of Whitefish Bay. Scheife's count, completed

Jefferson Park Pavilion, where school classes were first held prior to the construction of Whitefish Bay's first school building. *Whitefish Bay Historical Society.*

in March of that year, showed seventy houses and 312 people. A petition accompanied by the census was submitted to Judge Johnson, who on May 10 signed the order bringing our village into existence. Officials were elected on June 5.

One of the first orders of business for President Fred Isenring was to appoint a school committee. They prevailed upon the owners of the triangle now bounded by Idlewild, Fleetwood and Marlborough to donate the tract for a new schoolhouse. These owners were cagey, however, for they put a stipulation in their conveyances, which said that title would revert to them if the building was not started within six months. Fortunately, this never happened, for the Village Board authorized the expenditure of $4,500 for construction, which figure had to be increased to $6,600 when all the bills came in. 'Twas ever thus when one starts to build. Needless to say, the Whitefish Bay kids that fall did not trudge miles to school. Instead, they had classes in the Jefferson Park pavilion on the site of the present Henry Clay School until it got too cold for comfort. Then school adjourned to the side room in the Scheife grocery store, located where the Raydon Store now stands. The new school building was completed in late spring and dedicated on June 23, 1893. Mrs. H.K. Curtis, the first teacher, received the princely sum of $60 a year while Nicholas Rix, the janitor, got $75. Need I comment?

Having disposed of the school problem, the new village board turned to other pressing matters. Peeved at Whitefish Bay's secession, the Town of Milwaukee tried to compel village residents to continue to pay the town poll tax, which had to be worked out on the town roads. The village board countered by instructing constables George Rodd and Henry Scheife (here he is again) to arrest and punish any town officer trying to enforce the poll tax. The liquor license fee was set at $500 for three years. The first one was issued to none other than Prexy Isenring, who also doubled in brass as the lessee of the Whitefish Bay Resort, but he got his license at a reduced rate because his bar was open only during the summer. Even so, the license take must have been substantial, for in April 1893, an ordinance was passed directing that all liquor fees be used for poor relief.

In 1895, Dr. T.W. (for Thaddeus Warsaw) Williams succeeded Isenring as president. In addition to being an MD, Williams was active in Whitefish Bay real estate, had written a book entitled *Philosophy of Life* and was regarded by many as sort of an iconoclast for having had the temerity to deride the poems of Ella Wheeler Wilcox, the Edgar Guest of her day. Well, I have read one of her priceless gems written after a trip to Milwaukee and a visit to the old Lueddemann resort situated where Hubbard Park is now located.

The first verse of this rhapsody in rhyme reads:

Like crimson arrows from a quiver
The red rays pierce the water flowing
While we go swimming, dancing, rowing
To Lueddemanns on the river.

To get back to Dr. Williams' first term as president—he served again from 1900 to 1903. In 1895, the board really got in some good licks with the following ordinances:

- Unrestricted roaming of animals
- Protection of bird life
- No bathing in public waters
- No fortune telling—twenty-five-dollar fine
- Limit of two pounds of gunpowder per person
- No tying of animals to shade trees or lamp posts (did we have a parking problem even then?)
- Maximum speed (for horses, of course) a moderate trot.

No ordinance on auto speed was passed until 1907, when the scorching limit of twelve miles per hour was set.

The next year, H.A. Croft was elected president, and thereby hangs a tale, possibly apocryphal but nevertheless amusing. Croft ran a resort on the north side of Bellevue Boulevard, the earlier name for Lexington Boulevard. Apparently to ensure his election, he is said to have invited a number of soldiers on maneuvers at the armory on the south side of Henry Clay to be his house guests for the eleven days required by law to qualify them as Whitefish Bay residents and, consequently, bona fide voters. Needless to say, he won.

The later years had their share of interesting governmental actions and experiences, but I'll have to pass that up except to mention the extended donnybrook between Father Dietz and village president Frank C. Klode over the naming of Santa Monica Boulevard; or the time Klode, determined to sell what remained of the old Grams farm to the village for a park, stepped down from his office for an hour while the board took official action.

Changing street names seems to have been one of Whitefish Bay's most popular outdoor sports—and not once but sometimes twice and even three times. For example: Ardmore was once Battery Place and before that was Barrett Avenue. Circle Drive started out as Fernwood Place, then became Woodland Circle and then Wellington Circle.

Our Village Board did not always have such nice quarters as they have now in the new portion of the present village hall. During the first year, they met in the east room of the Scheife store for which they paid a rental of $25 per year. After the new school was built, they met in the second-floor assembly room until the first village hall was acquired in 1903. This building had a curious history. It was originally erected on the north side of Lexington Boulevard, east of the tracks, for use as a saloon. (Yes, they called them by that name in those benighted days.) But the high license fee of $1,500 per year put the honest tradesman out of business. For a while, the building stood vacant, and then it was rented for use as a church. (Now there's a switch if I ever saw one!) The village bought the building in 1903 and moved it to the north side of Fleetwood Place just south of the school. In 1898, the village fathers must have been afraid of a crime wave, for they bought a tiny lot at Marlborough and Lancaster for a jail for the sum of $30. This was abandoned when two cells were added to the first village hall. After the present village hall building was turned over to the Whitefish Bay Athletic Association, it got to be a hangout for blackjack games and other objectionable practices. Lewis Scheife bought the old building and moved it to 314 East Beaumont Avenue, where it was remodeled and stands today as a very nice looking small residence.

In the late 1880s and early 1890s, Whitefish Bay was an isolated community. Green fields stretched from the north side of Milwaukee to our new village. East Milwaukee (Shorewood's earlier name) was not incorporated until 1900. Two of the old photos in the display were taken during the great blizzard of 1898 on the Dummy Line right of way looking north from a point near Hampton. In the one picture, you see nothing but a few farmhouses. In the close-up shot of the locomotive and the train crew, who is that debonair young chap with the mustachios? Why, our man Henry Scheife, of course.

Whitefish Bay's growth was made possible by a unique transportation setup. Forgetting the old Sauk Indian trail, which was pretty narrow and probably a trifle muddy in wet weather, the first route to the bay was the toll road. Charlie Andrews, proprietor of the Newhall House, saw the pleasant lake vistas stretching northward and determined to open up these vistas to the people of Milwaukee. In 1869, he formed the Lake Avenue Turnpike Company and obtained a state charter to operate a toll road. Built at a cost of $50,000, the new road was opened in the fall of 1872. Starting at what is now Lafayette Place, it followed the lakefront to the present Silver Spring Drive. The road was unique in one respect—it had only one tollgate, and

This house on East Beaumont Avenue was originally a saloon, before being used as a church, as Whitefish Bay Village Hall and as the location of the WFB Athletic Association. It was eventually relocated and converted to a private residence. *Whitefish Bay Historic Preservation Commission.*

Lewis Scheife's store. The Whitefish Bay Village Board first met here, using the east room shown on the left of the photograph. *Whitefish Bay Historical Society.*

The Dummy locomotive and crew during the great blizzard of 1898. *Whitefish Bay Historical Society.*

that at the city, or south, end. As the city grew, the lower part of the road was abandoned, and the owners donated the land to the city. The tollgate moved progressively northward to Bradford Avenue, a point north of Hartford Avenue and, finally, to Capitol Drive (formerly Atwater Road and Mineral Spring Road). Andrews' toll road was the first incentive for the development of the North Shore. One John Luck opened a small tavern near the north end—a sort of "First and Last Chance" and the progenitor of the famed Whitefish Bay Resort of later years. Lueddemanns on the Lake (now Lake Park), the old Milwaukee Country Club and numerous roadhouses and picnic grounds were early developments. The last part of the road was sold to the county for $15,000 in 1913, and the entire length of Lake Drive became the public thoroughfare it is today.

But for a long time, the toll road was a plain dirt road, and the dust, particularly on Sundays, was heavy. So the Pabst Company employed a horse-drawn sprinkling wagon to keep the dust from flying on the approaches to the resort. William Staffeld, who was the driver for some years, had a

View of a horse-drawn buggy traveling north on the Whitefish Bay Toll Road. *Whitefish Bay Historical Society.*

delicious sense of humor, for he had lettered on each side of the water tank this plaintive message:

'Tis my sad fate this dust to lay
While you drink Pabst at Whitefish Bay

Steel rails first came to the North Shore in 1874 through a fluke. The Milwaukee, Lake Shore and Western, building southward along the lake shore from Manitowoc, had planned to use the tracks of the Milwaukee and St. Paul Railroad on the west bank of the Milwaukee River for their right of way into Milwaukee. But somehow they did not make arrangements until tracks had been laid as far as the old Dickman farm, several blocks from the site of the Milwaukee Country Day School. An official of the MLS&W called on Alexander Mitchell of the Milwaukee and St. Paul but got a prompt turndown from the canny Scot, who couldn't see why his road should give a hand to a competitor. The chief engineer of the new road saved the day with a novel idea born of necessity. Why not strike for the lakefront and come down the bluff near North Point to a terminal on the lakefront? The idea was presented to the Chicago & Northwestern, which was looking for a route into Milwaukee for its new line from Fond du Lac. The two roads teamed up, met at Lakeshore Junction (just south of Capitol Drive) and from there ran on joint tracks to the depot on the lakefront. So, in effect, we have the revered Alex Mitchell to thank for this desecration.

But there was still another steam railroad in the history of the North Shore—the Milwaukee & Whitefish Bay Railroad, better known as the "Dummy Line." Actuated by the same motives that prompted Andrews to build his toll road, Guido Pfister and associates opened the new path in 1888. The tracks began at Farwell and North Avenues, ran north on what is now Downer Avenue, then by twists and turns eventually reached the terminus at Henry Clay Street in Whitefish Bay at the front door of the Whitefish Bay Resort. In its short life span of ten years, the Dummy Line had a happy history. Limited service was maintained during the winter for the growing population of the North Shore, but in summer, a twenty-minute schedule was provided for the crowds flocking to the numerous resorts and picnic grounds along the shores of both the river and the lake. The socialites bound for the exclusive Milwaukee Country Club rubbed elbows with the holiday crowds headed for such places as Mineral Springs Park, Welcome Park, Jefferson Park and the one and only Whitefish Bay Resort.

The Dummy Line passed out of existence when the Oakland Avenue streetcar line was extended to Silver Spring Drive in 1898. But somehow things did not seem the same. The clanging streetcar pre-staged the automobile, and the motorcar spelled the doom of the North Shore resorts. But even today, the spirit of an Indian, flitting along the shadowy Sauk trail that once traversed the North Shore, may yet bend a ghostly ear to hear the thud of a horse's hoof on the old toll road or the chug of the engine on the old Dummy Line of the long ago. Who knows?

The history of Whitefish Bay is one of realtors and resorts. There was no industry unless you consider fishing, which at one time meant those succulent beauties taken from the bay of the same name. Alas, today the housewife at the market or the restaurant patron asking for whitefish gets a product imported from the cold waters of Lake Superior. The first commercial fisherman at the bay was John Luck. He made a bargain with William Consaul for the right to fish off the shore of Consaul's farm, which bordered the lake just north of Silver Spring Drive. Later, the Consaul brothers and others did some fishing, but the heyday of the industry came in the 1880s when Lewis Scheife began furnishing the Whitefish Bay Resort with from three hundred to six hundred pounds weekly. He also sold fresh fish by wagon twice a week to wealthy east side residents in Milwaukee. The wagon started too early in the morning for patrons to be up, so receptacles were left in shady spots near the door with notes giving orders. Then the wagon went on to the Old German Market, where stand owners eagerly bought any remaining stock of fish for retail sale during the day. Lewis Scheife quit fishing in 1892, and while he had several successors, the industry declined and died out about 1920.

I stated before that Whitefish Bay's history can be written in terms of building booms and resorts. The enterprising Milwaukee real estate firm of Stone and Thomas platted Idlewild Subdivision No. 1 in 1887, which gives us and our neighbors, Dr. and Mrs. Gaffney, the satisfaction of living in the first subdivision on the north shore outside the city of Milwaukee. Earlier that year, the Milwaukee, Lake Shore and Western had purchased a tract of land that is now Cahill Square. Rumor had it that the railroad would build car shops and freight yards. This may have sparked Stone and Thomas' action. In any event, the resultant boom saw the subdividing of much of the village before the bubble burst in the panic of 1893. Even officials of the railroad were financially interested in real estate, and the road ran special suburban service to encourage prospective homeowners to buy lots in their subdivisions. But when those lots were all sold, the commuter service was discontinued…so the village got back at the railroad by threatening to

MAP OF HIGHLAND VIEW,

IN THE SOUTH EAST ONE QUARTER OF SECTION 33,

TOWN OF MILWAUKEE.

THIS delightful suburban residence tract is located at White Fish Bay. It is one hundred feet above Lake Michigan, and has seventeen hundred feet of lake front. It commands a magnificent view of the lake and of the city in the distance. The Milwaukee & White Fish Bay Railway runs through this tract on the west, and its depot is located just across the road, affording the greatest convenience for residence purposes, with quick communication with the city.

Bellevue Hotel and Park, owned by Capt. Pabst, join it on the north. The new docks and steam-boat landing are almost directly in front of this property, and boats run regularly to and from the city. Lake Avenue, a macadamized road, runs through this tract on the east and north, and with its natural beauties of scenery, is one of the finest drives in the world.

Parties residing on this property, have the advantages of living on the Bay near the steam-boat landing, on Lake Avenue, and near the depot of the White Fish Bay Railway, advantages for beauty of scenery and convenience which are destined to make it one of the most desirable and popular summer resorts in the country. On the south east of this tract there are a number of mineral springs. The water possesses properties equal to the medicinal springs of Waukesha, iron and sulphur predominating.

The banks along the shore of the lake are composed of a valuable clay, which has by a number of tests, been proven to possess qualities for making fine stone-ware.

Several gentlemen, who have investigated the matter, have become enthusiastic over the prospect of turning this clay to a practical use. For plats and further particulars apply to **I. H. LOWRY, 82 Michigan St**

13

Advertisement from a real estate brochure that presents the advantages of living in Whitefish Bay. An illustration of the Pabst Whitefish Bay Resort, and its Belleview Pavilion, can be seen at the top of the map. The road just south of the resort is the present-day Henry Clay Road. *Whitefish Bay Historical Society.*

make the road put a watchman at every crossing in the village. The road compromised by agreeing to stop all trains, even the "limiteds," on signal at the Whitefish Bay station, located on the south side of Silver Spring.

For a while, Whitefish Bay was indeed a realtor's paradise. Everyone got into the act. George Rogers trumpeted loud and long in his newspaper. I quote from the January 16, 1892 issue: "No real estate investment is more certain than those in lots of the various plats around Whitefish Bay. One sweet cool breath off Lake Michigan is worth the price of a lot and nothing, absolutely nothing, is charged for the scenery."

These plugs for a bigger community contrasted strangely with the rural note of some of the local news items on the same page:

Mr. Remington's new barn is completed.
F.G. Isenring is the owner of a new team of roan carriage horses. These, with a new cutter and buggy recently bought, fix Fred out for winter and summer.
The village graded streets and put in wooden curbs and sidewalk.

C.R. Gether, in his subdivision at Day Avenue, went so far as to install private water and gas systems and ran a sewer to the lake. Tweedy built a water plant and sewer for his subdivision along the lake just south of Silver Spring, but after one case of typhoid attributed to a contaminated well, the sewer was abandoned. A total of twenty-five subdivisions were platted by 1893. It wasn't all speculation, for a number of new houses were actually built. You can still see some of them even if their faces in some cases have been lifted. You can usually tell them by the high basement walls and the use of cut stone for these walls. When the 1893 panic ended the boom, things got plenty rough. Lots that had sold for as high as $1,000 could be bought for the proverbial song. Some residents were *not* averse to tearing up curbs and sidewalks on vacant streets for use as firewood.

But Whitefish Bay, like the rest of the country, eventually pulled out of the depression and began growing again, but this time on a sounder, if slower, basis.

Gas street lighting had been installed in 1903, and Billy Mohr was paid ninety dollars per month to light the 141 lamps. Billy lost his job in 1913, when electricity replaced gas after a spirited election in which the vote was sixty-six for electricity to forty-four for keeping the gaslights.

By 1910, the population had increased to 812. About the time of World War I, the bungalow craze swept the country, and you can find a number of them in our midst, although we did not get anywhere near as many as Shorewood. The second real boom in Whitefish Bay real estate began in the mid-'20s. Many new subdivisions were opened. As the population grew, residents complained about the speed of the trains and the annoyance of the whistles, which, according to state law, had to be sounded at each crossing. An official of Whitefish Bay heard that the C&NW (which had purchased the MLS&W in 1893) had given up any intention of using its Whitefish Bay property for car shops and might be receptive to the idea of selling. He confirmed this at the Chicago offices and also found that the railroad would consider the abandonment of the line between Lakeshore Junction and what is now Fox Point, provided the villages of Shorewood and Whitefish Bay would jointly buy the old right of way. Because of the intense rivalry between the two villages, the Whitefish Bay man foresaw the trouble if Shorewood thought that the idea originated in Whitefish Bay. Accordingly, this official and the railroad concocted a plot whereby the Shorewood officials were "tipped off" that the C&NW might remove its tracks. The Shorewood group eagerly went to Chicago to present the proposal. The railroad officials, as the story goes, were properly reluctant but finally permitted themselves to be sold, and the project was ensured. Work started in 1927, and the last of the rails was removed by 1929, leaving Whitefish Bay with no noticeable flaws as a residential area. Since then, the growth of our village has been steady, and today the number of vacant building lots can almost be counted on the fingers of one hand.

And so we come at long last to the other potent factor in the early history of Whitefish Bay—the resorts. John Luck, who had opened his thirst emporium near the terminus of the toll road, sold to William Burr in 1872. Burr became so interested in becoming a boniface that he quit his Milwaukee clothing business and built and opened the Whitefish Bay Hotel in the summer of 1873. We read in the *Milwaukee Sentinel* that there was a grand picnic and ball on July 4 with music by Steins Band and with buses—horse-drawn, of course—leaving the corner of Spring and West Water Streets.

Some ten years later, Dr. Williams built a resort place called Fernwood Cottage on the north side of what is now Lexington Boulevard. In 1886, he leased it to Fred Isenring, who operated the place for many years, although the name was later changed to Edgewood. Henry Scheife (what, again?) told me that he worked there as a boy setting ninepins for bowlers

Fernwood Cottage, located on the north side of Lexington Boulevard. The name of the cottage was later changed to Edgewood. *Whitefish Bay Historical Society.*

and working back of the bar, where his diminutive stature amused the customers. But the biggest weekend in Whitefish Bay history began on the evening of June 25, 1889, when more than three hundred distinguished guests attended a dinner celebrating.

I believe the event he is referring to was a visit, sponsored by Pabst, of the "Ancient and Honorable Artillery Company of Massachusetts."

And what happened to the school that started this whole story? It served for twenty-five years until it burned to the ground in 1918. During that quarter century, it was a more or less unwilling mecca for enterprising kids who, on their way to or from school or at recess, carved their initials on the silver beech trees across the road. And that, I believe, is where we came in.

Chapter 2

OCTOGENARIAN TELLS OF LIFE IN EARLY BAY

ARTHUR RABE TALKING TO THIRD AND FOURTH GRADERS AT CUMBERLAND SCHOOL, 1974; RECORDED BY KAY LAPP

This chapter starts with a speech that Arthur Rabe gave to students at Cumberland School. It is followed by some early memories that he recorded. Through these and other efforts, Rabe did a lot to help preserve the early history of the village.

When I was five years old and my sister, Lottie, six years, my dad talked to us one day. "Whitefish Bay has no school!" He told us it may take a long time before the Bay has a school. "I want you kids to learn something so you won't have to work with tools, digging ditches or be out in all kinds of weather, snow, rain and cold."

So Lottie and I walked two or more miles to the Port Washington Road School. It was a Town of Milwaukee school. [It had] one room for boys and one room for girls. It was on the west side of the street, on William Lindwurm's Land. There were no automobiles in those days. Traffic was light and safe to cross the street.

It was a "no go." The weather did not allow us to go regular every day, and time was wasted. A lot of people that had children old enough to go to school had quite a few meetings about a school. George Rogers, [who] edited and printed the [*Whitefish Bay*] *Pioneer* weekly newspaper, said, "I will help all I can." He had four children ready for school.

More meetings, and then Rogers said, "Let us work to get to be a village and the school will follow." Henry Scheife was told to take a census of the people living in the Bay. His census showed there were 316 people living in the Bay. That number put us way over the top. They selected a committee

WHITEFISH BAY PIONEER.

DEVOTED TO WHITEFISH BAY AND VICINITY.

VOL. I. MILWAUKEE, WIS., SATURDAY, JANUARY 16, 1892. NO. 1.

MILWAUKEE LAKE SHORE & WESTERN R'Y.

CARD.

FRED. G. ISENRING,
PROPRIETOR,
WHITEFISH BAY PARK
AND
Whitefish Bay Family Resort,
WHITEFISH BAY, WIS.

LAWN GRASS.
Clover and Grass Seed.

A FEW POINTERS.

A petrified elephant has been unearthed near Jasper, Fla.

The value of land in Berlin has increased 85 per cent in the last ten years.

The wettest place in the world is at Cherra Poonjee, in the Khasi hills of Assam. The fall of rain for a single month has ranged from 100 to 200 inches.

MANAGER HILL'S MUSCLE.

When He Drinks It Is Likely to Get Him Into Trouble.

The accident by which J. M. Hill broke his leg will probably have the [illegible] of Mr. Hill for some time to come, say the N. Y. *World*. He is rather a short man and nothing about him indicates unusual strength. His muscles are well developed, however, and he has extraordinary ideas of his own physical power. Whenever he drinks he immediately begins to exhibit his strength. He nearly choked a man to death in Cincinnati some time ago, attempted to break another man's arm in an up-town oyster saloon and was vigorously thrashed for his efforts. Then he got into a row with a man named Foster at the Imperial Hotel, which resulted in Foster being whipped by another man, and so on through a series of pugilistic adventures. Finally he struck a snag of large, robust and overwhelming proportions. This snag was [illegible] Muldoon, the wrestler. Mr. Hill was walking along Twenty-sixth street one night surreptitiously and proudly feeling of his biceps, when he discovered Muldoon leaning nonchalantly against a railing. The manager and Muldoon were great friends and hence Mr. Hill thought it would be an admirable scheme to exhibit his muscle. He stepped forward and suddenly twining his hands in a handkerchief which was loosely knotted, around Muldoon's neck, began to squeeze violently. Muldoon started back and if he had not stooped down the two men would have gone over the railing together. The big athlete was

January 16, 1892 issue of the *Whitefish Bay Pioneer*, a weekly paper devoted to "Whitefish Bay and Vicinity." *Whitefish Bay Historical Society.*

to meet with Judge Johnson of the circuit court, who signed the order that brought the Village of Whitefish Bay into existence.

Tweedy Land Co., Richard and Elizabeth Burke and John and Catharine Mann, for one dollar each, deeded enough land to the village to allow for the building of a schoolhouse, toilet facilities and a children's playground. John Kohlmetz was chosen to build the schoolhouse. It was finished building in 1892 and dedicated in 1893. Unfortunately, this school burned to the ground in 1918. No cause of the fire was ever found.

A class of four graduated from this school in June 1900: Helen King, Earl McDougall, Norman McAllister and [me], Arthur A. Rabe.

The school you boys and girls go to, the "Cumberland School," is on ground that used to have cows, horses, wagons, plows, hay forks and much more. There used to be a well to draw fresh water, with a pump on it, for the house and kitchen needs. This well was near the house. Another deep well was near the barn so water would be available to the horses, cows and chickens. No doubt a large barrel was available to catch rainwater from the roof of the house because this rainwater was softer and used for washing clothes. Henry Schreiber and his wife, [who] owned this farm, had a family of boys and girls that were very helpful as they grew up. Young Henry was fifteen years old; Eddie, thirteen; Rosie, eleven; Minnie, eight; and Elsie, two years.

When Mr. Schreiber got up early in the morning, the first thing he saw to was that the animals were watered and fed. He then started to milk the cows, no doubt helped in the milking by the two older boys. As to watering the cattle, [the] deep well near the barn had a trough so arranged that the cattle could be drinking from both sides of the trough. After being milked and fed, in summertime they were put out to pasture. Now the farmer and children and wife were ready to have breakfast.

Then the farmer hitched up a horse to a wagon, put a can of milk on it—possibly ten gallons—took his measuring can and a bell to call the customers as he arrived in Milwaukee. No doubt he stopped at a butcher shop so as to bring home some fresh beef meat. No doubt he stopped at a bakery to bring home one or two coffee cakes, or pies, and even bananas to the gang. When he got home, of course, the family sat down to eat. Then,

Charles Rabe Homestead at 4856 North Woodruff Avenue. The farmhouse was originally located at East Chateau Place and North Marlborough Drive but was relocated in 1886 because of its proximity to the Chicago and Northwestern Railway tracks. *Whitefish Bay Historical Society.*

depending on the season, he would plow a field for planting potatoes or cut some grass to make hay for the horses and cows. There was always plenty to do. In rainy weather, every wagon, buggy, grass mower, etc., was taken to a shed, wheels taken off and plenty of axle grease put on to stop any screeching noise. The greasing had to be regularly done.

With a large herd of cows, you might have one that acted kind of ornery. My grandfather said take a board that had been fixed to be about two feet long and two feet wide and fastened on the cows horns. That cow could see the ground and grass but would not try to jump fences. It had to behave. Cows would sometimes get their milk bag dirty, and it was necessary to wash off the dirt to keep the milk clean. I believe the Schreibers also fattened about six pigs every winter and killed them one as needed, made sausages, etc., and the hams were well smoked in the smokehouse.

My folks, the Rabes, had three cows. After having been milked in the morning, it was up to me—about five years old [at the time]—to see to it they got to the pasture, which is right across the road from you.

[When] Mr. Krause died, Mrs. Krause sold barn, horse and everything worthwhile to Otto Runge, who had just been married, and all was moved to the east side of the railway tracks. The railroad bought the Krauses' eight acres, and the Rabes rented them from the railroad for cow pasture and used the rest for raising other worthwhile material.

Near Hampton Road, Krause had quite a few apple trees of all kinds and cherry trees. It was a question if I would eat the cherries or the birds, who were also waiting. The Rabes sold many a bushel of those apples and, of course, ate some.

The Rabes had a good friend, Gilbert Schultz, [who] worked in North Milwaukee and needed a horse and buggy to get to the job and back again. Schultz had a cow pony called Nellie. The horse had been branded on the right shoulder. Schultz told my father Nellie was getting too old and how about my giving you Nellie and [her] harness. "Let you boy and Nellie get acquainted, and he could ride Nellie." My father agreed to take the horse. Nellie and I got acquainted, and I rode the horse home with the cows.

In wintertime, the cattle and Nellie stayed in the barn. When a man or boy is around a horse, it is best to be careful. One evening, my father was milking our three cows, and I was told to water Bill, one of the horses. I got a full pail of water from the well and did a very foolish thing. Instead of saying, "Get over, Bill," I touched Bill, who had his head down in the manger. Bill with hind legs in the air shot me and the empty pail through the open barn door and landed me on the manure pile outside. I did not get hurt, but my

This 1876 map of the southern portion of what is now Whitefish Bay shows the ownership of the various parcels of land. It was drawn by Arthur Rabe, based on his recollections. In his narrative, Arthur Rabe speaks of the properties near what is now Cumberland Grade School, including those owned by his parents, by Henry Shreiber and by Mr. and Mrs. Krause (Kruse on the map). *Whitefish Bay Historical Society.*

father might take care of that. I quickly got a full pail of water and said, "Get over, Bill," and Bill got his drink. It must have gotten by my dad, for he said nothing. But I was extra careful after that.

Rabe also told the children of excursions to Pabst's Whitefish Bay Resort, noting that since his father worked there, he was frequently able to get free ice cream. He stated that the ice cream for the resort was made by the turning of the Ferris wheel. After Rabe finished his talk, it is reported that he was surrounded by students with more questions.

In a separate interview, Arthur Rabe provided the following additional memories of growing up in Whitefish Bay:

I speak now how tough it was to live in Whitefish Bay, long before the Dummy Line. We had no electricity. We had kerosene lamps for home and barn lanterns. The people living on the south side [of the village] near Hampton Road had a long walk to get to Louis Scheife's store [on East Silver Spring].

It is true we had a mixed group of German, Irish, Polish, etc. We had quite a few residents that had money, were well fixed with good jobs and could afford a horse or two and a buggy to come and go all the way to Milwaukee and back. Farmers had horses and could help themselves.

The farmers raised assorted vegetables, had apple trees, raised corn, potatoes, wheat and rye grains for bread baking. They produced eggs and butter. All was used to feed [their] families and sell the balance to have some money coming in to buy clothes, shoes, etc. Money also was needed to buy a wagon, buggy, horse or cow.

They had to have a real knowledge of things. Wheat and rye had to be cut down and tied in bundles and made to stand up for about four or five days of curing. There were no binders in those days. The farmer learned to make a binder out of wheat or rye straw. When he got [the bundles] into the barn, he had a real job to do. Many dictionaries show a picture of a flail—the kind they made themselves.

The flail had a stout piece of wood about six feet long with a large hold at the end to let a stout leather strap through to fasten this onto another piece about four feet long. They laid a bundle of grain on the barn floor, and two men [stood], facing each other. When the first man had whacked down on the grain, the other man raised his to whack down. Thus, they took turns flailing away. When they had quite a little straw on the floor, they had to remove it. It was used for animal food. Then, with broom and a large sieve, [they] shook it well and removed the dirt from the kernels of grain.

Illustration of two farmers using a hand tool called a flail to thresh[1] grain. *Sackett & Wilhelms Litho. Co., 1892.*

In looking over the residents shown by the census of 1892, it is apparent to me that a very large group of men lived near the Rabe home near Hampton Road. Many of

Men working in the Milwaukee Cement Works stone quarry. The two men on the right of the photograph are breaking up rock with sledgehammers. Presumably, the rock pieces were then carted away and taken to the cement works, where they were broken into small pieces and fired to produce cement. The original plant was located on the east bank of the Milwaukee River, just south of Hampton Road. The lagoon in Estabrook Park is the site of one of the partially filled quarries. *Whitefish Bay Historical Society.*

these people, the men, were employed by the Cement Mills at Humboldt Avenue and Capital Drive. I remember the Cement Mills well, as I was there during the summer vacations. The Village of Whitefish Bay needed a lot of stones, gravel, etc., to keep our roads in shape. We had four or five teams of horses to go to the mills and get waste material that the mills did not want. In summertime, the wagons loaded with three yards of waste material had to climb up a road I believe was a forty-five-degree angle.

When the horses had pulled the load halfway up the road, they needed a rest and breather. The driver would be ready with some large stone or wood and block the wheels so they could not move backward. After the horses started the load again and got to the top, they were allowed another breathing and resting spell.

In vacation, my father had me doing the driving as I only weighted about sixty pounds. You could see the horses and road from on top of the wagon—better than walking aside of the load. I was about six years old.

Chapter 3

FISHING THE BAY

First Commercial Enterprise in Whitefish Bay

This article describes a journalist's excursion to see John Luck's fishing operation in July 1862. It was published in the Milwaukee Sentinel *on July 17 of that year.*

Five minutes' pull brings you to the pounds; a few minutes' inextricable twisting of ropes, ducking of heads and, in our case, a continual chorus of nautical phrases, in which all joined and above which the horse laugh could be heard loud and distinct.

After getting in sight of the web, the doors are shut and the net pulled up, so as to bring the fishes near the surface. The sight is well worth seeing. The water becomes alive with the finny creatures, all wiggling, gliding and squirming in an almost solid mass of tails, heads and fins. Thousands of the silvery herring, the plump, scintillating white fish, the broad flounder, the succulent bass, the rank sheep's head, the great sluggish sturgeon, the pickerel and many others, all massed in a living community. The visitors are allowed to haul out all they want, which is easily done, as they (the fish) are so congregated that they can be caught with the hand.

The scene is an exciting one, and Mr. Luck, who owns the nets, takes great delight in the interest shown at his unique exhibition. Parties always come to shore with selected strings of fish for which a mere nominal fee is charged.

On our arrival, a party of gentlemen was observed, accompanied with ladies, who had just been out to visit the pound.

The scenery in the vicinity is picturesque and the locality pleasant.

A pond net fishing operation, similar to that of John Luck in Whitefish Bay. *Drawn by L. Kumlien for the* Review of the Fisheries of the Great Lakes, *1885.*

In 1938, Mary Jane Consaul Scheife (Mrs. Lewis F. Scheife) of Whitefish Bay wrote a summary of fishing in the bay for a historical research project. Her account serves to remind us of where the village got its name.

John Luck put in the first pond net in Whitefish Bay in 1862, getting his fishing rights from William Consaul and setting up "shop" at Silver Spring Park—the east end of Silver Spring Drive at Lake Drive—down on the beach. After two years in this location, John Luck moved to the beach approximately at the base of present Circle Drive and fished there for ten years. The fish were sold locally.

William Consaul and his brother, Captain Theodore Consaul, then started fishing—hiring William DeYoung of Green Bay to help get the fishing nets started. William Consaul built his own boats (he had been a shipbuilder)—a twenty-four-foot flat-bottom boat and a fifteen-foot boat. Fish were sold right on the beach when they returned from emptying the nets. Mr. Consaul fished off Silver Spring Drive for about eight years, and then his son, William T., and a neighbor, Frank Koje, took over the fishing business. Alphas Elliott helped them dress and pack the fish.

Typical commercial fishing in Lake Michigan using pond nets. Notice the pulleys used to pull up the nets. *Milwaukee County Historical Society.*

After several years, they sold their nets and boats to Lewis Scheife and Charlie Langschwager, who took up the fishing business. They moved the landing place about five blocks north of Carl Sheife's beach—Carl was Lewis' father, and their land was in the approximate 6200 block of North Lake Drive, so they were fishing just into what is now Fox Point.

At this same time, Fred Isenring put in a net at approximately the foot of Henry Clay Street or a little to the south, but a storm tore up his net, and he sold to Otto Doman, who fished only through one summer.

After four years of fishing, Lewis Scheife bought out Charles Langschwager's share and furnished all the fish for the Whitefish Bay Resort. [He sold the resort] three hundred to six hundred pounds of fish a week. He would also go out twice a week in his wagon to both the city and countryside to sell fish. He fished for eleven years, quitting in 1892.

In 1899, Pete Schaefer bought Mr. Sheife's nets and used the same landing. He died in 1920, and in 1921, Frank Klode bought the nets and started fishing—more for the pleasure than for business. He stopped about 1924, and that was the last of the pond net fishing in Whitefish Bay.

Chapter 4

THE 1862 INDIAN SCARE

STORY BY MARY JANE CONSAUL SCHEIFE

This story was originally published in the Milwaukee Journal *on August 9, 1930. It was written by Mary Jane Consaul Scheife about an "Indian scare" in 1862. Interestingly, the panic was widespread throughout Wisconsin. The scare apparently stemmed from an incident in New Ulm, Minnesota, earlier that year in which several bands of Eastern Sioux (also known as Dakota), trying to drive whites out of the area, attacked settlements in the Minnesota River Valley. It doesn't appear there ever was any spillover into Wisconsin.*

On September 3, [1862,] we were living with our parents in Whitefish Bay. The farm extended from what is now Richards Street to the lake. Our house was built of logs, just as most of the houses were in those days, and was located on Silver Spring Drive, about one hundred feet east of Lake Drive.

On that September day, my three sisters and I were playing in the front yard, while Father and my older brother were working around the barn, when suddenly we heard shouting. We ran to the gate and saw two men on horseback galloping up the road, waving their hats and shouting, "The Indians are coming! Everybody go to Milwaukee!"

Of course, we were frightened, and Father was particularly worried because Mother was in bed with our baby brother, only three days old, and he thought we would have to stay. A dear old neighbor woman was staying with Mother, helping with the work and taking care of the baby. I was not quite four years old, but I remember hearing her say to Father, "Now, William Henry, the best thing for you to do is to take your family to Milwaukee to your sister Lydia's and stay a few days." Mother also thought this would be best. "Go down to the barn and turn all the stock out in the pasture and lock the doors," she continued, "for if the Indians do come they will set fire to the buildings. By the time you are back with the horse and wagon, I'll have Ruth and the children ready."

She then ordered us all to get busy and collect our clothes. There was no time to pack suitcases or boxes. Everything was tied in small bundles, and in a few minutes we were ready.

Mr. Everts, husband of the neighbor woman, and another neighbor came in and helped Father fix a bed in the back of the wagon. Mother and baby were made comfortable in it, surrounded by bundles and pillows. Father and we other five children sat in front, and we started our long drive down the Lake road. Mr. Everts and the other neighbor loaded guns and stayed to see what might happen.

The Lake road was not much like the Lake Drive of today. Then, it was only a narrow trail, with woods on either side and only a few log houses between Silver Spring Drive and the middle of Lake Park. At that point, there was quite a large house and picnic ground where city people used to picnic.

Our aunt lived on Biddle Street, near Broadway. It took us a long time to make the trip, for Father drove slowly, and I think the old horse was not much of a speeder at its best. But eventually we did arrive.

Aunt Lydia saw us coming and ran out to meet us. The first words were all settled, with Mother and the baby snug in bed. After supper, our cousin took up to Juneau Avenue to see the soldiers drill.

The next morning, Father and two men who lived in the house next door to Aunt Lydia started out to Whitefish Bay with the horse and wagon to see what had happened during the night.

It was a long day for us children waiting for them to return and expecting to hear that our home had been destroyed. Our cousin took us down to the old market square to see a company of soldiers march down East Water Street. I think they were ready to leave the city, for there was a big crowd of people cheering and shouting goodbye.

Father and the other men came back just before dark and reported that everything was all right. No Indians had appeared. When, early next morning, some of our neighbors drove in and said that the Indians had left their camp near Cedarburg and started for Green Bay, we went back home.

The morning after we returned, Father and some of the neighbors were sitting on a pile of logs in the yard, telling stories and talking about the scare. I remember hearing Father say, "I think it would be a good plan to go

This interesting photograph shows people escaping from the Indian massacre of 1862 in New Ulm, Minnesota, pausing to eat dinner on the prairie. The photographer is thought to be Adrian J. Ebell. *Library of Congress Prints and Photographs Division. Wikipedia Commons.*

into the woods and shoot some squirrels to get these guns cleaned out." Mr. Everts laughed. "I think," he said, "that those guns wouldn't be much good for the table. We loaded them to kill Indians, not squirrels."

Three of the children who made the drive to Milwaukee for protection that day are still living in Whitefish Bay on different parts of the old farm. They are Mrs. Susan Consaul Marsh (140 Silver Spring Drive), Mrs. Mary Jane Consaul Scheife (118 Beaumont Avenue) and Frank Consaul (2424 Richards Street).

Chapter 5

INTERESTING WHITEFISH BAY TALES

TOLD BY MARY JANE CONSAUL SCHEIFE

This article was originally published in the Whitefish Bay Herald *on June 4, 1942. It provides an account by Mary Jane Consaul Scheife of life in the 1800s in the area that is now Whitefish Bay. Mrs. Scheife had passed away the previous December.*

Mrs. Lewis Scheife (née Mary Jane Consaul) was born in a log farmhouse within the limits of Whitefish Bay. Her parents were William Henry and Ruth Shoulder Consaul, who came to Milwaukee in 1847 from Toledo, Ohio, and settled on a thirty-six-acre farm on the site now bounded by Santa Monica Boulevard, Silver Spring Road, Lake Michigan and Elliott's farm on the north.

The Consauls bought this thirty-six-acre tract from a Mr. Lipscomb. On it was a log house where the couple made their home and also a small frame house where Mr. Consaul's father and mother lived until their deaths. Mrs. Scheife says life in the early days was not difficult, although they knew nothing of the conveniences and luxuries of the present day. Her father worked his farm, raising mostly garden truck and enough hay and grain for their stock and cattle. Some grain was sent to the Plerron mill for grinding, and later on, grinding was done at the Bender mill. Mr. Consaul had been a first-class shipbuilder in the East, so had no difficult[y] in securing work during the winter at the old Wolf and Davidson shipyard on the Menomonee River in Milwaukee. This work, together with the pound fishing operations they carried on in the bay, produced ample cash income for their needs while the farm provided a comfortable home and a great plenty of vegetables, fruits, berries and meat.

Mary Jane Consaul. *Whitefish Bay Historical Society.*

Three Families

At the time the Consauls moved to the bay, there were but three American families living in the vicinity—the Charles Everts, their son-in-law Sylvester Abbey and Humphries. The Everts had a farm in the north end of the present village, the Abbeys lived in a rented house on the Everts farm and Mr. Humphries, a gardener by trade, lived on what is now Sylvan Avenue and later moved to New York. Mrs. Scheife says the Abbeys were gone for two years on a trip by covered wagon to Pike's Peak, during the "Pike's Peak or Bust" days. After their return to the bay, they soon moved to Saginaw, Michigan, and later on to Tennessee.

Mrs. Scheife well remembers Anson W. Buttles, who for fifty years was clerk in the Town of Milwaukee and whose sister married Paul Juneau, a son of Solomon. Two of the daughters of this couple, Anna and Marion Juneau, where married to Henry King and James McGee, partners in the large Milwaukee printing concern, King, Fowle and McGee.

Recollects Wildcat Scare

Mrs. Scheife told of the following incident that occurred when she was a young girl. One day, a neighbor came running to her home much excited over having seen a wildcat on his farm. Mr. Consaul pulled on his boots, took down the gun over the door and, rounding up other neighbors similarly armed, chased the wildcat until they lost it in the woods and without getting close enough to shoot.

During Mrs. Scheife's childhood, there were no churches closer than Milwaukee, and she had to walk daily to the school located on Port Washington Road, about a half mile north of Silver Spring Road. Later, the town school district was divided, with one school located on Port Washington Road near the Green Tree Road and the other, called the Lindwerm School, on the Port Washington Road near the golf links in the present Lincoln Park. There was no high school closer than Milwaukee.

For recreation, they had frequent parties, birthday and anniversary celebrations and an occasional trip to the city for an evening at the theater. The German [families] also held picnics and dances at the several taverns located on Port Washington Road.

Train Snowed In

The second winter the railroad ran through the Bay, the southbound train was snowed in at about where Lake View Avenue now is, from about 3:00 p.m. on Friday until 2:00 p.m. the next day.

About six o'clock, the conductor sent two of the crew with a note to Mr. Consaul asking if he could furnish supper for eighteen passengers. The men got lost in the storm, and instead of going east, they went to the Port Washington Road. That was at the end of the Silver Spring Road, east of the river in those days. Inquiring there at a little house, the men were told by the old man resident that the Consaul home was located three-quarters of a mile east. Facing the storm, the two messengers walked the distance and arrived at the house about eight o'clock, and when Mr. Consaul let them in, they looked more like snowmen than human beings. While the conductor's note was being read, the Consaul boys brushed the snow from the men's clothes. Then, all busied themselves in the making of supper. About ten o'clock, a large clothesbasket lined with white oilcloth and paper was filled with food and covered by tablecloth. The hot dishes were well packed, and a six-quart pail of coffee was included. In addition, there was milk, cream, a basket of dishes, knives and forks, spoons, sugar, salt and pepper. Mr. Consaul and two of the boys helped the men carry the baskets and pails back to the train, where it was received with great enthusiasm, as some of the passengers said they had not eaten since early morning.

The next day, several of the passengers walked down to the Consauls' home for breakfast and stayed the morning and amused themselves by reading and playing dominoes until the train was able to continue on its way.

Mr. Consaul and his son William were taken to Milwaukee on the train to buy groceries and were brought back on the evening train. The C&NW railroad later recompensed Mr. Consaul with a liberal check.

In 1886, Mary Jane Consaul was married to Lewis Scheife, a native of Germany who immigrated to Milwaukee County with his [Pomeranian] parents at the age of nine months in 1856.

MOVE TO THE BAY IN 1866

The elder Scheifes moved from Milwaukee to the Bay in 1866 after the Civil War, through which Carl Scheife served in the Union army. They first lived on a farm near the present Country Day School, extending from Santa Monica Boulevard to the lakeshore. Carl Scheife was a farmer, carpenter and bridge builder and helped to build the first Chestnut Street Bridge in Milwaukee. As young Lewis grew to manhood, he worked with his father on their farm, and when about twenty-two years of age, he formed a partnership with Charles Langschwager and entered the fishing business. Their nets were spread off the beach off his father's farm. A large scow was rigged with a pile driver for driving the net stakes. The weight, about two hundred pounds, was attached to a rope, which a crew of several men would pull and suddenly release, the falling weight driving the stakes solidly into the lake bottom. Pound nets[2] were used and a sort of fish trap rigged with nets. When it was thought a sufficient catch had been made, the men put out in a large flat-bottom rowboat, lifted the nets and scooped the fish into the boat. Their catch would consist of sturgeon, perch, lake bass, lake trout and whitefish. A goodly part of their catch went to supply the Pabst resort for its famous fish dinners, while a wagon route for the benefit of city customers along Prospect Avenue who liked fresh fish and a stand in the old German market in Milwaukee completed the market for their fish.

As the modern fishing laws were enacted, which would have forced them to set their net much farther out in the lake and probably make necessary the purchase of a steam fishing tug, the business was discontinued, and Lewis Scheife, in 1892, entered the grocery business, having his store and home on Silver Spring Road at Lake Drive, a site now occupied by the Whitefish Bay pharmacy and Krause's grocery. Here, Mr. Scheife conducted his store for eight years when he gave up that business and started up a hardware store on Silver Spring Road, in which business he continued until 1920,

Lewis F. Scheife owned the first store in Whitefish Bay, located where Winkies presently stands. Mr. Scheife died in 1946. *Whitefish Bay Historical Society.*

when he retired. Mr. Scheife was the second treasurer of the village, being elected to that office for the years 1892 and 1894. Again in 1904, he was elected treasurer, and his incumbency lasted for fifteen years until his retirement from active business life.

During the years Mr. Scheife spent in the grocery business, he was postmaster of Whitefish Bay, which position carried with it more honor than profit. He says that many months he received as much as sixty or seventy cents remuneration, or the sum total of the postage stamp cancellation of the office.

[At the time this story was originally written,] Mr. Carl Scheife, still hale and hearty, physically and mentally at the age of eighty-seven, [was] living with his son Al W. Scheife and family at 5055 North Berkeley Boulevard. Another son, Henry, [lived] at 5933 North Berkeley Boulevard. Mrs. Scheife passed away in December 1941.

Chapter 6

MEMORIES OF THE BAY

BY LAURA WEBER FUNKHOUSER

This June 1980 letter from former village resident Laura Weber Funkhouser was prompted by a meeting on the history of the village conducted by the Whitefish Bay Women's Club. In addition to describing early life in Whitefish Bay, it sheds some insight into the fire that destroyed the Fleetwood School.

We moved to the Bay in 1912. At that time, our address was 204 Connecticut Avenue—now 828 East Glen Avenue—and occupied by Mrs. Marie Fox. Connecticut Avenue was only one block long, running from Lake Drive west [and] stopping at the streetcar tracks just east of the Northwestern Railroad Depot.

Cause of the fire that burned the school was due to a very strong east wind blowing hot ashes and chips of wood from a train and engine that was going north at about 7:00 a.m. The railroad tracks were just across the street from the school, at Pennsylvania Avenue. Arthur L. Weber of Connecticut Avenue was one of the first persons to notice the fire. We called the village president—I believe it was Mr. Isenring—but by then others noted the fire, too, and called in. When there was a fire—even in 1916 or 1917, and later too, it was the rule to get in touch with the village president first to get an okay, and then he would phone the fire department at Park Place near Oakland Avenue. Then the fire engines, driven by several large, strong horses, would make the run out to the Bay. But by the time they reached their destination, whatever was burning was all burned. Or it was burned too badly to have been saved or salvaged.

Recent picture of 828 East Glen Avenue. *Whitefish Bay Historic Preservation Commission.*

The water situation in 1912 [consisted of] an artesian well[3] at the foot of Silver Spring Drive and Lake Drive. This well served only the people along Silver Spring—east from Pennsylvania Avenue, Glen Avenue Lake Forest and Birch Avenues. Other homes in the nearby vicinity—Day Avenue south or north—had their own wells or water systems. Everyone had rainwater cisterns until water was piped in from Milwaukee.

The village erected a flight of stairs with four double benches along each side of the way down to the lake. This was at Silver Spring Drive and Lake Drive. As there [was] no bathing house at the foot of the stairs at the lake, your home was your bathing suit dressing room.

South of Birch Avenue the area was heavily wooded—was wet and marshy—where many, many wildflowers grew, and there were many wild strawberries, raspberries, gooseberries, and it was a birds' paradise.

It is a pleasure to reminisce about the Bay as it was then—surrounded by farms to the south, the west and the north of its boundaries; and to compare it with the beautiful Bay of today. We enjoyed it in our earlier years—and are still enjoying it many, many years later.

Chapter 7

RECOLLECTIONS OF LIFE IN EARLY WHITEFISH BAY

BY HEPHWORTH WILHELMINA ISENRING KERBY

The following article was based on an interview with Hephworth Wilhelmina Isenring Kerby, originally taped on September 6, 1892, by Mimi Bird and Judith Kloman. During her sometimes-rambling interview, Hephworth discusses the first two presidents of Whitefish Bay. The first, her uncle Fred Isenring, disappeared in 1899 among allegations he had absconded with funds from the Milwaukee County sheriff's office.

I was born at my home, 1012 East Colfax on November 2, 1899. Dr. Thaddeus Williams was my doctor. In 1913, he saved my life.

I was attending a box social at the Methodist Church on Silver Spring. I was very interested in the church and Sunday school—I'd won a Bible in a contest. My mother fixed chicken and everything, and I went to the box social. Mother didn't go, and we were playing and having a lovely time before things were being served. You bid on your boxes, and whoever bid on your box, you were his or her guest. Anyway, we were playing "Wink," and they had those big heavy kitchen chairs. Walter Backman pulled the chair out as I went to sit down, and I fell and hit my back and passed out—just like that. They picked me up and put me on a cot. Finally, I woke up, and I said, "Oh, my back!"

So they took me home. They carried me halfway home down the block. We were living at that time in Doroqowski's house[4] on the other side of the tracks, while our house at 1012 East Colfax was being built. They brought me to the backdoor, and my mother said, "What are you doing home?" I started to cry and said, "I got hurt, I got hurt!" They got me in the house and told her what happened. So mother put me into bed right away. They had a bedroom right off the living room. That was a big house; the railroad tracks went right alongside it—there was no road then. So right away my mother put hot applications on my back and spine.

My father was superintendent of the county poor office in Milwaukee, [located] on Market Street, so he called Dr. Lemmon, who was the county doctor. He said, "Bill, just put hot applications on it and I'll come out in the morning." He came out in the morning. He wasn't very gentle. He took me and rolled me, and I let a yell out of me, and my mother thought the roof was falling through the house. Dr. Lemmon said, "Bill, I'm going to take her into the hospital—we're going to operate."

My father said, "You're not operating until we know what's wrong." The doctor replied, "All right, Bill. OK."

Old Doc Williams lived across the street in that lovely home there, with his daughter and Kitty, his niece. My dad said, "Hephworth got hurt." Doc said, "I'll be right over." Doc then was seventy or seventy-two years old. He came over, and I was lying on the couch, and he turned me very carefully, and I said, "It hurts so, don't touch me, just let me lie." My father took a gib

Recent picture of the home of Dr. Thaddeus Williams, 942 East Sylvan Avenue. *Whitefish Bay Historic Preservation Commission.*

quilt and put it on the dining room table and put extra boards in and put a quilt over it, and he laid me on my stomach.

Dr. Williams went up and down my spine so gently, and he felt it all over. I was all black and blue. He said to my dad, "Anyone who wants to operate, they're crazy." He went to the telephone and called Kitty and said, "Kitty, I'm sending Gladys over, and I want you to give her a jar of that ointment that I make up and some tape and gauze." Gladys was my sister. So she went over and got the things and brought them over. Dr. Williams worked on me and pressed and, every time he touched me and it hurt, just said, "That's going to be all right; it'll be all right, just let me do it." And I just loved him—we all did.

So, he said, "All right." He took the ointment and put it all over my back, put gauze over that and put tape all around my lower back and abdomen and down my leg. My right leg became paralyzed—I suffered terribly. They carried me back to the couch. Dr. Williams said to my father, "Bill, put a few boards on this couch. If she wakes up, or happens to turn in her sleep, one of the discs are going to slide out. You call me right away."

At three o'clock in the morning, he called the doctor. Dr. Williams came over there right away and said, "That's all right; I'll have to make the tape tighter." So he pulled it off, reset it again and put the tape tighter, like a regular corset. And that's the way I laid. I laid for three months like that.

I received no pain medication. They didn't give you anything in those days. A little whiskey they might give you, but I was only fourteen. So I laid that way.

He made a little arched thing that, two weeks later, he started to examine my spine with. He went over every vertebra with a little rubber mallet, and he pounded each vertebra, [saying], "Easy, real easy." But he knew what he was doing all the way down my spine to the end of that tape. Then he said, "Tomorrow I'm coming over to see how she is, but I'm not going to bring the mallet. I'm going to every other day give her treatments like that." And that's finally what released me.

He said to my mother (he called her "Min"), "I want you to, everyday, to get her up and swing her legs down, otherwise she's going to have more troubles." I was flat in bed all the day, but once a day they'd get me up.

The man I [eventually] married, Harold Kearby, a Scot, was a brakeman on the railroad. All the railroad men (the engine used to stand around on the "Y" to help pushing trains over the siding, pulling them in) said, "We're all going to take our turn; we're going to get her on her feet and get her walking." And every day those men came over. I only weighed eighty pounds at the time. My [future] husband was one of those who came over. They'd stand in front of me with their back to me, and they'd loop their arms through me and say, "Now we're going to walk—left, and right." But the right one didn't work so good, but they'd say, "Walk, walk, walk." Sometimes two at a time would come—even the dispatcher came over once.

It took about three months for the right leg to come back, but it did come back fine. I've had back trouble ever since, though.

Dr. Williams said, "I want you to go every morning on the streetcar to the Kryzch's farm, over the railroad track. Go in the barn where they're milking, and you drink that warm milk." I did that for six months, day after day.

Kitty Williams was a wonderful person. Grace Williams was Dr. William's daughter. She was a spoiled brat. His wife had died a number of years back. I don't remember her at all—she died long before I was born. I think that Grace was an adopted daughter, and Kitty was a niece who came from Kentucky.

Doc Williams had an office downtown on Wells Street in Milwaukee. He was not a tall man, but he was well built, and he took good care of himself. I always thought he was the best-looking man in town. He gave me a ring that had belonged to his wife. It has three diamonds and two blue stones in it. I'd wear it once in a while. It's a beautiful ring. I was a special patient to him. He always called me, "My baby." He brought all my brothers into the world.

My oldest brother was Wynand, then Archibald, then Gary, then Clarence, then Gladys (1896), then me (1899), then Alice (1902). Alice was born in Milwaukee; the rest of us were born right here in that house on Colfax.

Dr. Robert Peterson, the dentist, has an Aunt Edna, who married Clarence. After Clarence died, Edna married Archie. My brother [Clarence] was a World War I veteran. He got that gas—he and Max Belau. He had a horrible death.

My mother was Minnie Peters. She lived in Milwaukee before she lived here. Her youngest brother, Henry, had a farm on the Silver Spring Road. Her oldest brother was Fred. She had a sister, but she died of some rare disease. The farm was kitty-corner from where the White House Inn used to be on Port Road. The Hickmans lived in there. I went to school with LaVerne Hickman out there in Whitefish Bay.

I was a baby when Fred Isenring disappeared in 1899. Fred was my father's brother—a good-looking man. Nobody ever found his body. We all thought somebody maybe did Fred in. I was never in Gallus Isenring's [Fred's father] home; we were gone by that time. The folks decided to move into Milwaukee because it was better for my father's work. With the trolley, if you missed one train you had to wait another hour. Many a time I walked from Schweke's home, which is now where Bayshore Shopping Center is located, home because we'd missed the train.

Anna Isenring was my father's oldest sister—my Aunt Anna. Anna married David Milbraith. Mary was his second sister—she married Carl Schober. The Hoppenraths built a house right next to us on Henry Clay Street. Anna lived always in the front house, and Mary lived in the house behind—on Meadow Place. Her daughter, Willa Johnson, still lives there in that house on Henry Clay. Our house was right next to the railroad tracks.

I was so surprised by Whitefish Bay. The last time I was here was in 1919, when I got married. We had a great big wedding at the Armory. We had big tables. Mrs. Immekus baked all the wedding cakes. My father did several nice things for them. They were having problems. My father was one of them kind—he always helped everybody. The wedding reception was held inside. I was married in our house. At that time, Colonel Westfahl and his family were living in the house on the Armory grounds. He had three girls. The oldest girl ran around with my older sister, one with me and one with my younger sister. We always were together. They lived in the Langlois home—that's what they called the house on Briarwood.

I never saw my grandmother Maria. She died before I was born, but I can remember my grandfather [Gallus Isenring]. He had a beautiful white mustache and beard. It was just like silk. How I used to like to go and comb it. I'd say, "Grandpa, can I feel your face?" And he'd say, "You sure can, honey." Grandpa met Grandma on the boat from Switzerland, and when they got to this country, they got married.

I was a little girl when Grandpa died. He always said, "Grandma was waiting for me." She died just before I was born. [Grandma] said, "I hope that we have a little girl, and I want her to be named Hephworth." Too bad I don't remember that. I'd have said, "Don't put that handle on me!" They named me Hephworth Wilhelmina Isenring—Wilhelmina after my grandmother and Hephworth after Fred Isenring's first wife.

I had black hair—black as coal—and it was kinky, but it got curly as I got older. My mother was a wonderful cook. She took good care of us. My dad was the same way. But we respected our parents. You didn't talk back or say, "No, I'm not gonna do it." We went to the Methodist Church.

The boys used to walk down the railroad track every morning going to school. [They] had a great big St. Bernard dog. That dog took the boys to school and waited if they played out[side during recess] 'till the school bell rang and the boys went into school. Then the dog would come home. At three o'clock, as soon as the clock struck three, Bruno would be going down the railroad track to go and get the boys from school.

The school was the one that burned down in 1918, near the Kryzch farm. Kryzch's farm was just north of the school.

I remember the resort. You know, every summer they would hire a band that would come in and spend the whole summer there and play. They had a Ferris wheel, and the boats used to come in from Chicago down to the pier and unload the people. My dad and mother would take us over—we'd go and sit and listen to music. They had meals there, too. We'd always get an ice cream cone. They'd bring it on a little plate, and the cone would be tipped upside down. Then you'd take it and turn it over, and there was your cone.

One year they had the Tyroleans. Was that marvelous! They were a singing band. They were all complete musicians, and every one of them would sing too. A lot of times Daddy would take us up, if we behaved, and if mother didn't have any complaints about the children. They had a space where people could dance if they wanted to. One wing went out that way, and one went out that way and in the middle was a big stage. The long walks that went down to the lake—I went down one of them with a boy's bicycle. They were gravel walks down very steep hills. It was five o'clock one morning. There I am, my bad sleeping habits—I don't sleep good. I was up all hours of the night. I used to get up and go downstairs in the basement and play with my puppy. [Anyway], I went and stole my brother's bicycle. I could ride that thing like a little speed demon. I went down that hill. This was way before I had the accident. I must have been about ten years old. I went down that hill—I kept the brakes as hard as I could.

When I landed, I landed right by the water. I didn't fall off the bike. I got caught in the sand. Then I had to push the bike all the way back up. When I got home, my mother said to me, "Where have you been?" I said, "I took a ride down to the lake."

"You what? Well, that's enough! You're not going to do *that* again. Wait until your father finds out—you're going to get it!"

The Pabst Whitefish Bay Resort, from an old postcard, looking north toward the Ferris wheel. *Whitefish Bay Historical Society.*

The Tyrolean singers first came to America for the St. Louis World's Fair in 1904, when it is reported they "scored a tremendous success." They then toured the country with their show, which featured singing, dancing and yodeling. *From an early 1900 playbill.*

I said, "Do you have to tell him?" She told him, and I was punished. I was sent to my room all day. I was locked up many times.

I had lots of friends to play with. We had kids that we went to school with—farmer kids—the Bauch family had a bunch of kids. Neighbor kids would come to the yard, and we'd play. We had a great big merry-go-round where we lived, right across the field. A big one! My father got it going. Some guy didn't want it, so he bought it and set it up. A real merry-go-round from some carnival outfit. All the kids came over and said, "Ahhhh! A merry-go-round!" It had horses that went up [and down] and tubs—like a tub you sit in. It had a gasoline motor in it to make it go. The kids all liked to come over. We all had a lot of fun.

I also played with dolls. I have four of them now that are being fixed. They had beautiful china faces and kid bodies. I have one of the first jointed dolls that came out, with her hat and red dress and her patent leather shoes. I've been offered money for them, but I'm saving them for my granddaughter, who loves dolls. I combed their wigs so many times!

I remember when they opened the new school (Henry Clay—now the Middle School). Every weekend there was a dance in there. Everybody's family came. They served lunch and had a good time—no rowdiness!

Chapter 8

THE TRUTH ABOUT WHAT HAPPENED TO CHARLES McGEE IN 1903[5]

A Horse Driven to Water

The McGees lived in the northern of the two homes called locally the "Whitefish Bay Twins," located on Lake Drive just south of Silver Spring Drive. The two nearly identical homes were constructed in 1893—one for the McGees and one for the Kings. The two families were related—Anna Juneau McGee and Marion Juneau King were sisters and granddaughters of Solomon Juneau, the founder of the city of Milwaukee. They were great-granddaughters of Jacques Vieaux, a French Canadian fur trader and the first permanent white settler in Milwaukee. The following story is about Charles A. McGee, son of James and Anna McGee, who was twenty-nine when the events occurred.

Inching along a freeway at rush hour or totaling up his annual repair bills, a Milwaukee driver may suppose that traffic problems are strictly a modern phenomenon. The problems are different now from what they were on a 1903 afternoon, when Solomon Juneau's great-grandson went for a drive—no doubt about that. Charles A. McGee didn't have to contend with such things as freeway tie-ups.

On the other hand, the horses under the hoods of cars can be depended on to avoid one hazard McGee encountered. None of them will take a notion to jump into Lake Michigan and head for Muskegon.

McGee's widow, Anna,[6] who will be ninety next March, has supplied details of that exciting drive of nearly seventy years ago. Mrs. McGee, whose father, Adolf Meyer, was president of the Cream City Brewery, was then a sophomore at Milwaukee-Downer College, and she wasn't aboard the buggy that day—but she's heard all the details.

McGee, who later served as Milwaukee County district attorney, seconded Robert M. LaFollete's presidential nomination and ran for governor of California, was married to Anna's sister [at the time].

After [Anna's] sister died of a ruptured appendix, leaving two young daughters, Anna and McGee were married. One of the daughters grew up and married John McCone, who became Atomic Energy Commission chairman, [followed by being named] director of the Central Intelligence Agency.

But on the June afternoon when McGee headed north on Prospect Avenue in his carriage, all this lay in the future. With him were his daughter, Betty (three), and his brother-in-law, John (fifteen). The plan was to go to Milwaukee-Downer, where his wife was having lunch with her sister. Then the McGees intended to head to North Milwaukee for a family gathering at the home of Mrs. McGee's uncle, Anson Buttles, who was celebrating his eighty-third birthday. McGee drove east on the avenue named for his great-grandpa, then turned onto Prospect.

Automobiles were beginning to share the streets with horses, and one of them followed close behind the carriage. The tailgater seemed amused at McGee's efforts to hold back his horse, which was threatening to run away. Just as the motorist turned off on Kane Place, the horse took bit in teeth and started to run. McGee hauled back on the lines, [but] the bridle broke. Now totally out of control, the horse went galloping down the hill that in those days brought Prospect to the level of the Northwestern Railway tracks.

"I heard a train coming and saw the tender lower the gate at the crossing," McGee said, according to his widow's recollections. "I turned to John and asked him to jump, [but] he had fainted." All McGee could do was push him to the floor, hoping the dashboard would protect him. "I took little Betty by the collar of her dress, leaned out of the buggy and dropped her gently on a pile of rubbish as we dashed by."

The crossing gate loomed close. The horse dashed under it, breaking loose from the buggy. McGee, who had been a University of Wisconsin football player before he became known as the "silver tongued orator of Wisconsin," filled his lungs and braced himself.

"I hit full force with my chest," McGee said, "breaking the gate off like a match stick. I was thrown against the moving train. My overcoat caught on a brake beam, and I was dragged fifteen feet or more before it tore and I fell—a few inches from the track. I felt as if I had been shot out of a cannon against a stone wall."

A trolley had stopped to wait for the train, and a doctor who happened to be aboard hurried over. He decided McGee had no broken bones and ordered him to go home to bed. Later, it was discovered several ribs had been cracked.

"I'll do no such thing," McGee told him and hurried off to see what had happened to his passengers. Both had been lucky. John was only bruised. Betty was unhurt but crying—partially because her nice white dress was dirty.

So far, you might say, the accident wasn't much different from something that could happen to a 1972 motorist whose brakes failed. But the kind of horsepower in fashion in 1903 had a mind of its own. McGee's horse, which had hit the [train], leaped up, snorting, and headed south along the railroad right of way. With bystanders pursuing and others running to intercept it, the horse galloped along the railroad right of way until it got to the Northwestern depot on the lakefront. A crowd had gathered to watch the excitement, and several men tried to grab the animal. But it shook them off. The horse had had enough of Milwaukee traffic. First, there had been that tailgating automobile, then the unyielding train. The animal wheeled, galloped out on the breakwater, jumped into the lake and headed toward Muskegon—where life was quieter.

The Chicago & Northwestern Depot on Milwaukee's lakefront during the era described in this story. *Whitefish Bay Historical Society.*

Someone at the Depot called the lifesaving station, and a crew launched a longboat and started chasing the horse—now nearing open water. The sailors caught up [with] the animal about a thousand feet beyond the breakwater, Mrs. McGee reports, and one of them grabbed the broken bridle. There was a considerable struggle, but eventually the men tied a rope to the horse and forced it to swim back to the foot of what was then called Wisconsin Street.

A man named Olsen was captain of the boat crew. After the crowd at the lakefront had finished cheering, Captain Olsen said he'd headed many a rescue expedition, but this was the first time he'd ever had to chase a horse that was heading toward the middle of Lake Michigan.

And so it all turned out happily that afternoon of 1903. McGee procured another buggy and took his wife to the Bittles' party. Some years after his broken ribs had healed, he went on to such further adventures as campaigning for Sherbie Becker against Dave Rose and assisting former president Theodore Roosevelt after Teddy was shot on Third Street [in 1912] on his way to the Milwaukee-Auditorium.

An early advertisement for the Milwaukee company owned by James McGee, Henry King and Alonzo Fowle. Fowle lived at what is now 624 East Day Avenue in Whitefish Bay.

Editor's note: James McGee was one of the earliest presidents of the village of Whitefish Bay. Henry Rousseau King served for a time as village justice of the peace. James McGee and Henry R. King were well-known Milwaukee businessmen, having owned a publishing company. They may have been the first daily commuters to live in Milwaukee. Along with their partner, Alonzo Fowle, McGee and King's company was among the first to print photogravures—high-quality photographs that reproduced the detail and continuous tones of original photographs. Their photogravure books are considered to be some of the earliest "coffee table" books.

Chapter 9

WHITEFISH BAY—MY HOME

BY MARY MCINTYRE

The following story of growing up in Whitefish Bay was submitted to the library as part of its "Personal History Project."

In 1931, my father and his family built in Whitefish Bay, moving from their home in Milwaukee. Three years later, my father, a veteran of World War I and director of the Veterans' Service Exchange, brought his Ohio bride to the new home. I was born seven years later, in 1940, and how lucky I was to grow up in the developing community of Whitefish Bay. Our home was half a block north of Richards School, and there were still empty lots close by to play in and explore. Klode Park was a half block to the east with the lake just beyond.

Most of our neighborhood families were young couples who had just built, and there were plenty of kids my age to play with. I remember Sandy Casper, who lived in a house that had been moved to Berkeley from Lake Drive; Mary Clare Hubbard from across the street; Cathy Hirschboeck, whose family lived on the corner of Montclair and Berkeley; and Roger Buffet, whose house was just down the block from us. Summer evenings we had neighborhood games of hide-and-seek and Red Rover, Red Rover. We girls enjoyed doll tea parties, dress up and playing school.

It was a short walk to kindergarten at Richards—a bit farther for first grade at St. Monica's school with nuns as our teachers. At that time, the church, now on the northwest corner of Silver Spring and St. Monica Boulevard (then Richards Street), was only a congregation's dream. Services were held

The McIntyre home being built in the 5900 block of Berkeley Boulevard in June 1931 for Edward and Mary McIntyre. The people pictured are relatives John and Fanchon Tuthill McIntyre and Clara Tuthill Bradley.

in what is now the basement of the present church, and much of the parish property was undeveloped—fields with old farm buildings.

Our family was a happy one, marred only by my father's chronic heart problems. My parents loved to garden, and (lacking TV) they read aloud to each other in the evenings. We'd go to the movies—pre–Fox Bay—on Milwaukee's east side or downtown and enjoyed eating at Eugene's or Karl Ratzsch's or, more often, the Yankee Doodle. Every summer, we'd vacation in Minocqua for a month or so, to indulge my father's love of fishing.

It was one of those vacations—when I was nine years old—that my father had a fatal heart attack. Thinking back, I wonder at my mother's decision to keep the house in Whitefish Bay, instead of moving back to Ohio. She was now the family breadwinner with a mortgage and small savings—living in the increasingly wealthy community. Having been a children's librarian in the Cincinnati system, she hoped for a position at the local library but found that the job included nights and Saturdays—not good hours while raising a child. Happily, Wilde's Pharmacy (later Bear's Reliable Pharmacy) was only a block away from home and hired mother as a clerk—later to take over billing for the business.

By sixth grade, I was found to have rheumatic fever and was tutored on and off for some years, even into high school. High school, of course, was

Whitefish Bay High—Holy Angels didn't exist then—a long walk along the then being constructed Marlborough Drive. Due to my frequent health problems and being something of a bookworm, I can't say I enjoyed much of a social life in high school—but the education was outstanding. I was readily accepted by Marquette University in 1959—going on to UW and UWM for a graduate degree in library science, a profession not only embraced by my mother but also by my great-grandfather, who had been Ohio state librarian.

While I was in high school and until my third year at Marquette, I worked part time at the Whitefish Bay Library as a shelver and circulation clerk. After getting my degree, I worked for a couple years in the Milwaukee City system, coming back to Whitefish Bay Library as a reference librarian in 1969—helping the village's residents with their research and reading needs, later with their computer needs, for thirty-six years until retiring in 2005.

After living in Whitefish Bay for thirty years, in 1970 we purchased an old farmhouse on three-plus acres in Mequon and moved out of the community. I so appreciate having grown up in such a safe, friendly place in those wonderful innocent years. Continuing to work at the library even after the move kept my connection with Whitefish Bay strong for sixty five years of my life.

I remember:

- The polio epidemic of 1944. At age four, I really couldn't understand why I couldn't play with other kids in the neighborhood, but due to an outbreak of polio in the Midwest, Wisconsin children twelve and under were confined to their homes.
- The "Big Snow" of 1947. The snow started on January 28, 1947, and continued until it turned into a blizzard with sixty-mile-per-hour winds and drifts of ten feet or more. According to a 2007 article on Journal Interactive, the city was paralyzed, and it took forty-six days to clean up. I remember a drift going almost to the second story of the next-door house.
- The "Professor" who was a brilliant recluse living in a ramshackle old farmhouse west of Lydell and just north of Silver Spring. We younger kids were terrified of him and the scary stories about the pond in his front yard. Later I found that, while normally solitary, he would coach students at the library in math or philosophy.
- A delightful and dedicated Mimi Bird, who had a passion for history. [She] researched all of Whitefish Bay's past and generously donated her materials to the library.
- A first glimpse of television in the '40s with a dozen TVs massed in a store window on Silver Spring.

Mary McIntyre sitting with her father, Edward Thornton McIntyre, in front of their Berkeley Boulevard home after the "Blizzard of '47."

- The old library in the basement of the then village hall on the southwest corner of Marlborough and Lexington with Mary Bowen president
- The "new" library built in 1955 at 5420 North Marlborough, where I worked as a "page"-shelver, circulation, etc., and where Jane Eggum was the library director. Jane was an "old-fashioned" director—not only managing the building, budget, staff and advocating for library interests with the village manager and Library Board, but also working all aspects of the profession from materials selection to collection maintenance to reference—a director whose door was always open and who treated her staff with a respect and compassion that evoked their devotion and dedication
- The gorgeous new expanded and technology-ready library built in 2001 under the supervision of the brilliant director, Tracy Biaschka. She and the other members of our staff were family—a team whose goal was to serve this wonderful community to the best of their ability.
- Memories of the holidays celebrated in Whitefish Bay. In the '40s at Halloween, there were parades and a judging of costumes at the high school sports field. I won three dollars with a third place wearing a tombstone costume built by my father. The Fourth of

> July in Whitefish Bay was always a major holiday with a parade. We joined in on bicycles and tricycles decorated with crepe paper. [There were] fireworks over the lake.

Whitefish Bay was then and is now a remarkable community. I feel privileged to have grown up and worked in the bay—also delighted for this opportunity to call up memories of those days.

Chapter 10

MOVING TO THE BAY

BY LOLITA R. BRUMBLAY, FEBRUARY 8, 2011

This letter was written in response to the Images of Whitefish Bay *book published in 2010. Lolita Roska Brumblay moved with her parents to the village in 1926. She initially lived with her grandparents at 5101 North Santa Monica Boulevard, until her parents' house was completed at 5841 North Shore Drive. Her letter provides an interesting look into the village's past.*

My son brought *Images of Whitefish Bay* to me—it brings back many memories. My grandparents Robert and Annie Kruecke were early residents of Whitefish Bay. When Grandpa's foundry, Kruecke Bros., which made brewery and bar supplies, went out of business because of Prohibition, they bought the Mittelstadt farm on the gravel road, Richards Street. It was a little north and across the road from the Leu farm. Sadly, Mrs. Mittelstadt, the original owner, had [hanged] herself in the barn on the property after hearing her son had been "killed in action" during World War I. The sturdy home is still standing at 5051 North Santa Monica Boulevard.

The farm extended from the Wittenberg home on the south (5035 North Santa Monica), north to Lancaster and west at least two city blocks. In 1932, my aunt Kruecke and Howard Kortsehl moved into their new "honeymoon home" at 5065 Richards Street, and Uncle Roy and Ann Kruecke had their home built at the southwest corner of Richards and Lancaster—all part of the original farm property.

In 1926, our dad, George J. Roska, was having a new home built for our family in Whitefish Bay at 5841 North Shore Drive. Our residence on Forty-

Number 5051 North Santa Monica Boulevard. *Whitefish Bay Historic Preservation Commission.*

first Street across from Sherman Park sold so quickly [that] we moved into the farmhouse with our Kruecke grandparents during the summer. An apple orchard was on the south side of the house with a vine-covered gazebo on the west side. A chicken coop and several animal pens extended westward, and the big barn was north of those. Rows of asparagus and fields of corn filled the western landscape. Hunting for eggs in the chicken coop was fun. Every now and then, a horse-drawn wagon with a vendor selling popcorn would come along the graveled Richards Street. Pennies Grandma gave me for dusting the legs of the dining room table and chairs found their way to that wagon.

In the fall, while still at the farm, dad took my brother, Junie, and me over to Henry Clay School to meet the principal, Mr. Mulrine, and signed us up for school. I was to be in Miss Hamilton's third grade class, and Junie was in the second. One day, my brother and I were ready to walk to school. A farmer was in the yard unloading feed from his wagon. We were ecstatic when the farmer asked us if we'd "like a ride to school?" He hoisted us up on top of the feedbags, and off we went with the horse and wagon along graveled Richard Street to Henry Clay School. The farmer drove the wagon right up on to the gravel schoolyard. All the kids who were there came crowding around the wagon. That day, as the farmer "unloaded us," we felt like royalty!

Richards School opened in October 1928. Being close to Halloween, we chose our colors to be orange and black. We had begun the school year at Henry Clay in a separate class along with the teacher and students who would soon transfer to Richards School. A dated picture of our fourth grade class at Richards School was taken. Then the grade school only went up to sixth grade. Seventh and eighth graders went back to Henry Clay. As my class progressed, seventh and eighth grades were added for us. My eighth grade class of 1933 was the first to be graduated from Richards. That fall of 1933, all four high school years were represented.

Often, Dad would take us kids to the Riding Academy in the southwest corner of Whitefish Bay on Fairmount. Bridle trails were in Estabrook and Lincoln Parks along the river. The Hays' home at the northwest corner of Day Avenue and North Shore Drive used to have two metal posts topped with horses' heads at their curb on Day Avenue where horses could be tethered.

By 1943, when this photograph was taken, the stairs at Silver Spring Park were severely undercut by beach erosion. They were abandoned. *Whitefish Bay Historical Society.*

The wide, wooden stairway going down to the beach [see image on page 69] was at the east end of Silver Spring Road at the intersection of North Lake Drive and Silver Spring Road. That spot was said to have been the "unloading area for Rum Runners from Chicago" during those Prohibition Days.

Dad and Frank Klode were friends who often played pool in our "Rec Room." Mr. Klode suggested that Dad might like to make a pathway down to the beach and keep a boat down there to go fishing. Dad did that. He took a long thick rope and wound it downward in a zigzag path, from tree to tree, until he had an easy path to follow to the shore. He kept a rowboat, over-turned, near the edge of the bank. I don't remember if he kept his Evinrude motor in a protected casing under the boat or if he brought it down whenever he planned to use the boat. One day, we came down to go boating, and a family, who had found our path, had their picnic lunch spread out on the upside-down boat—using it for a picnic table.

Eventually, Frank Klode gave the land Freddie Grams had reaped grain on for so many years to the village for a park. All the neighborhood kids played "Cowboys and Indians" on the mounds of black dirt being used to cover land in preparation for planting grass seed. Our dear mother didn't know where to start cleaning us up after we had rolled in that black dirt.

The [Klode Park] bank was contoured in two sections. It was sloped halfway down with lannon stone steps to a lannon stone path installed across the base. On the lower bank, a lannon stone path sloped downward parallel with the bank, from south to north, and a railing went all the way down along the lakeside. A few steps at the bottom turned toward the beach. One summer, WFB High had a "stand" at the beach to raise money for the band. Charles Belik's mother had charge of it. Before we had lifeguards at Klode Beach, Philip Farley drowned while rafting with Dick Lowe and Dorothy Miner.

Every winter, a large rectangular ice rink, parallel with Belle Avenue, was prepared. A seasonal warming house was put up to accommodate the skaters. Sometimes we skated there during gym class.

Tennis courts were put in. Until the Jaeckels built a home on Lake Drive adjacent to the tennis court on the north side, we could play tennis before school in the morning. Disturbed by the racket of the bouncing balls, locks on the gates were installed to be opened at 9:00 a.m.

The Leus' daughter married a black man employed as a chauffeur for a family who lived on Lake Drive. I miss my office files, which are "up north." I am trying to find out the name of this couple. I believe their children were the first of black heritage to attend the Whitefish Bay schools. One of the boys was elected president of his class.

It has always been my understanding that Whitefish Bay was named by Henry Scheife, noted fisherman. His granddaughter, Bernice, was in my class. Her married name is Zahn.

Chapter 11

IN THE 1930S, I WAS A LATCHKEY KID[7]

BY GLORIA ROCKWOOD HOUGHTON

This story helps illustrate what life in the Whitefish Bay business district was like in the 1930s. The author, Gloria Houghton, who grew up in the village, was a prolific storyteller. Several of her stories are included in this book.

A butter knife under the doormat in our apartment building was my latchkey to spring our lock in case my parents decided to lock our door.

My father was a pharmacist and owned the drugstore around the corner, and my mother managed the bookkeeping and penny-candy department for him. From fourth through eighth grade, I always knew where to find my parents, even though they didn't always know where to find me. Each day, I checked into the drugstore after school at 3:30 [p.m.], and I generally brought several friends with me because Daddy gave us the best root beer floats in frosted, copper mugs, and Mother let us pick out our favorite penny candy.

Then we would ride our World Bicycles up and down Lake Drive, enjoying the scenery that Whitefish Bay, a suburb of Milwaukee, provides. Traffic in 1934 was sparse, even on a main thoroughfare. There was one hill in the village, and we would pump our bicycles to the top and then coast down "no-handed" with our feet on the handlebars.

Some days we would roller-skate on Silver Spring Drive in front of my parents' pharmacy. One day I left my roller-skates in front of the store, and a woman slipped on them and fell. My father expected a lawsuit, and I expected a spanking. The lawsuit never materialized, but my first spanking did.

Gloria Houghton's dad, Ellsworth Warren Rockwood, owned and ran Ott's Pharmacy (center) in Whitefish Bay, located at 501 East Silver Spring Drive. *Whitefish Bay Historical Society.*

On rainy days, after checking in, my friends and I would use the butter knife to open our apartment door. We played checkers, Hearts, Monopoly, Pit and Politics, depending on the number of friends involved. Often, we played with our favorite Dionne Quintuplet paper dolls when there were five of us. We sewed clothes for our Shirley Temple dolls and taught each other about the virtue of French seams and bound buttonholes, which we never quite mastered. We experimented with my mother's makeup, lathering our faces with Pond's cold cream and putting orange Tangee lipstick on our mouths, thinking no one would notice.

In winter, Daddy replaced our root beer with hot chocolate at the soda fountain, and Mother stuffed our snowsuits with extra candy. We donned our sheepskin-lined stadium boots and headed for Klode Park with our sleds or Sears-Roebuck skis. We found that just rolling down the hill in the snow and making snow angels was the most fun of all. The city flooded the tennis courts to create skating rinks. Not all of us mastered the fine art of skating, and not all of us could defend ourselves from the barrage of snowballs that those awful sixth grade boys threw at us. When the streetlights came on, we knew that it was five o'clock and time to hurry home or we would miss the *Lone Ranger* and *Little Orphan Annie* on the radio.

After my favorite radio programs, I would retire to my "office," a shelf in the back of a closet. I would decode Orphan Annie's daily secret message with my special decoder pin. I had other important paperwork. I was a member of Colonel Roscoe Turner's Flying Club. The more cereal you ate, the more box tops you collected and the higher your rank rose in his Flying Club. My parents ate his cereal, too. So I must have been a five-star general, with all of the medals pinned on my sweater.

We were encouraged to play after school, and no academic homework was ever assigned except on weekends. Fifth grade introduced the girls to domestic science and the boys to manual training. In domestic science, we did have one homework assignment each week: cook one dinner for your family without using a can-opener. My daddy would take a dollar bill from the cash register, and my grocery shopping would begin. (If I had any change left over, I could keep it!)

I would run to Mr. Brand's meat market first. For twenty-five cents, I could get either one pound of round steak ground, three slices of liver, three lean-loin pork chops or three large Usinger's hot dogs. Sometimes Mr. Brand would give me a free soup bone to make vegetable soup. After deciding on my entree, I would go to Sendik's vegetable market. I would buy three large baking potatoes for fifteen cents and three handfuls of green beans or another vegetable for fifteen cents. A head of lettuce cost twenty cents, and a tomato was five cents. I had spent eighty cents when I headed for Mrs. Meredig's Bay Home Bakery. I always asked for one-fourth-dozen dinner rolls. After all, I was in fifth grade, and we were studying fractions in arithmetic. My shopping was complete, and I had five cents in change for my

Gloria pictured with her parents, Bud and Florence Rockwood, while on vacation at Pelican Lake, Wisconsin, in 1930. *Deborah Houghton Schmidt.*

efforts. My daddy always brought home a pint of Neapolitan ice cream, so I didn't need to worry about a dessert.

Using our trusty butter knife, I let myself into our apartment and started cooking. I phoned my parents at 6:00 [p.m.], and they hurried home for dinner, and then Daddy returned to the drugstore for the evening. One time when I was cooking, I bought two eggs, wrapped them in flannel and hid them under the dishtowels in the drawer. I wanted to produce my own chickens. Several weeks passed before my parents smelled a terrible odor in the kitchen and discovered my rotten eggs.

Mother and I spent wonderful evenings together while she supervised bathing, shampooing, storytelling and prayers. Then she tucked me into bed at nine [o'clock] and went back to the drugstore. She and my dad would close the store and empty the contents of the cash register on the counter of the soda fountain. They would roll the pennies into red, cardboard tubes from the bank and make out the deposit slip for the day's receipts. They would put the money into a tan canvas bag, turn out the lights, lock the store and walk two blocks to the Whitefish Bay State Bank, where they deposited the money into the night depository. They knew that Mr. Swan would find it in the morning and return their deposit slip when he came to the drugstore for his morning Alka-Seltzer and Coke. When my parents returned to our apartment, they thought that I had been sleeping, but I was reading a Nancy Drew book or Madelyn Brandeis travel book under the covers with my flashlight. When I heard their footsteps, I stuffed my books under my pillow and tried to fool them.

Time passed quickly those five years of my latchkey life. No one had a happier childhood. My friends and the root beer floats increased until there were eight of us. We called ourselves the Linger-Not Kids. By seventh grade, our game playing turned into Auction Bridge. We loved to play bridge at our apartment because there were no parents to tell us what we were doing wrong with our bidding or why we shouldn't trump our partner's ace. We were the Linger-Not Bridgers then.

At the end of eighth grade, a strange thing happened. Boys on bicycles began to ride in circles under our apartment windows while we were trying to concentrate on our bidding. It was then that my parents decided that the latchkey days were over.

They bought a lovely, large, English-type home one block away and installed a housekeeper. In 1938, housekeepers cost seven dollars a week, plus room and board.

I was encouraged to continue to bring all of my friends home, male and female, but there was always someone dusting the picture frames or

Soda Fountain Counter at Ott's Pharmacy. *Whitefish Bay Historical Society.*

repolishing the silverware in the next room. When we went downstairs to the recreation room to play "Deep Purple" or "Stardust" on the 78rpm Victrola, there was always someone who decided to do laundry in the adjacent room. A stolen kiss would have to come much later in another venue.

My latchkey butter-knife days were over. I thank God for my beloved, wise and thoughtful parents.

Chapter 12

WHERE IN THE WORLD IS FREDERICK G. ISENRING?

BY JEFF AIKIN, CHAIRMAN OF THE WFB HISTORIC PRESERVATION COMMISSION

This article was first published in 2008 in Bay Leaves, *Whitefish Bay's community newsletter.*

Given his real estate and civic activities, it could be argued that Frederick G. Isenring did more than anyone to develop the village of Whitefish Bay. He helped incorporate the village in 1892, served as first village president from 1892 to 1895, represented the village on the Milwaukee County Board, developed three residential subdivisions, sold land to the Pabst Brewing Co. that became the Pabst Whitefish Bay Resort and then operated the resort for the brewery before becoming sheriff of Milwaukee County.

But on Christmas 1899, at age forty-five, Fred Isenring and $20,000 of Milwaukee County funds—an amount equal to more than $800,000 today—vanished, never to be seen again. Where did he go?

Fred was the son of Gallus and Wilhelmina (Zetteler) Isenring, and he may have been born in Whitefish Bay. His parents met on the ship that brought them to the United States, and the couple worked a farm for eleven years at what are now Lakeview Avenue and Shore Drive before moving to Milwaukee.

Fred became a businessman active in Whitefish Bay real estate, insurance and loans. His ads read, "Whitefish Bay Real Estate a Specialty." He acquired a parcel of lakeshore land, later sold it to Pabst for the resort and then ran the resort under lease from Pabst.

Fred married Hepworth Chandler, and they had two children, Mary and Hattie. Hepworth died in 1894. Fred remarried and had another child, Mildred, who was a baby when Fred disappeared.

Frederick G. Isenring. *Whitefish Bay Historical Society.*

The house that Isenring constructed for his family at 920–22 East Sylvan Avenue was originally built next to the Village Hall on Fleetwood Place in 1892. Dr. Thaddeus H. Williams, the village's first health officer and a business associate of Isenring, acquired the house after Isenring went missing and relocated the stately residence to [East] Sylvan Avenue.

Originally a single-family home, the house was later subdivided into a duplex. The house was recently razed. The owner donated an ornate stained-glass window, which is prominently displayed at the Whitefish Bay Library.

After leaving office as village president, Isenring served a term as Milwaukee County sheriff from 1896 to '97. While sheriff, a depression caused the bottom to fall out of the real estate market, putting Isenring in financial trouble. It was later discovered that $20,000 in funds were

The Morning Herald - Dec 27, 1899

TO ARREST AN EX-SHERIFF

Milwaukee, Wis., Dec. 26.—An order for the arrest of the former Sheriff of Milwaukee county, Frederic C. Isenring, was issued today. Isenring completed his term on January 1 last, but up to the present time has not rendered an accounting of the last half year of his incumbency.

A writ of mandamus was served upon him recently to render such report, and his failure to comply resulted in the order for arrest.

Mr. Isenring has been prominent in Republican politics in this county for several years and served as chairman of the Board of Supervisors for one term. Nothing can be stated at this time as to the condition of his official accounts during the latter part of his term.

PANIC IN CARACAS.

This newspaper account about the missing ex-sheriff was published in the *Morning Herald* in 1899.

missing from the Sheriff's Office, and an order was issued for his arrest. A few days before Christmas 1899, and while supposedly en route to Fond du Lac on business, Isenring disappeared.

Where did Fred Isenring go? His family believed he may have committed suicide, but rumors persisted through the years that he had fled to Puerto Rico or Alaska or other global points. One story had him headed south to start a wine business.

Chapter 13

GROWING UP ON DAY

FROM THE JOURNAL OF JOHN WILLIAM SULLIVAN

The following is an extract from a booklet written and published by "Jack" Sullivan. The author grew up in Whitefish Bay and lived for a time on East Day Avenue.

We moved [to the Bay] from Fox Point in the fall of 1917. My brother Bud, as we called him then (his real name is Eugene), and I rode on the wagon that carried some of the furniture to our home on Day Avenue, which my folks had just bought. This was a large eleven-room house with a large screened front porch. There were four rooms and a large hall on the first floor, with an open stairway to the second floor. There was a living room, parlor, dining room and large kitchen. A natural fireplace was located in the parlor. The second floor had five bedrooms and a bath. The third floor had two finished rooms plus the attic space. On this floor [was] a huge storage tank that held the water that was pumped up there by our windmill.

Everybody had windmills at that time to pump water from the well to the tank in the attic. We later got city water, and then the windmill was dismantled.

We lived in this home until 1928. The home on Day Avenue was numbered 16 when we moved into it. The number was later changed to 146, and I believe that now, since the North South, East and West were added to the numbering system, it has been changed again to [516] East Day Avenue.

I have many pleasant memories of the time spent on Day Avenue. My youngest brother, George, was born there in 1919, so I was no longer the baby of the family. Day Avenue ran from the lake west to Richards Street

Number 516 East Day Avenue, where the Sullivans lived between 1917 and 1928. This photo was taken in 2012. *Whitefish Bay Historic Preservation Commission.*

(which is now named Santa Monica Boulevard), a distance of about four or five city blocks. There were enough kids on this block with just the boys to have our own baseball and football teams. The Wiggins had four kids (two boys); the Glasers had five kids (two boys); the Sullivans had five kids (four boys and one girl) with two of the boys of an age to play together—Bud and I; one was younger and one older. The Klattes had five kids (two boys our age); the Bucks had three kids (two boys); the Kraemers had fourteen kids (about four our age).

We used to practically live at the beach during our younger years. We would pack lunches and go and stay all day. When we were younger, my sister, Margaret, kind of watched out for us. If she was there to look after us, we could go anywhere. Besides playing football and baseball, we would have carnivals and sell lemonade. We all had paper routes, and I can remember my sister, Margaret, delivering her papers in a baby buggy with baby brother George in the buggy. The customers were few and far between, and for these few customers, we had to travel miles. I remember my brother Bud's route; he had about twenty customers yet had to walk close to four miles a day to deliver his papers. I wonder how many kids would do that today. I was younger, so my route was shorter—about a mile and a half or two miles.

While living on Day Avenue, I started my schooling at St. Robert's Catholic School in Shorewood. From the years of 1918 to 1920, there were the four of us going to this same school. We would all pile into the Model T Ford coupe, and Dad would take us to school and drop us off on his way to work. I don't know how we all piled into that car—four kids and Dad with our books and our lunches—but we did it. We always got excused from class at 3:15 p.m. every day so we could catch the 3:30 streetcar to Whitefish Bay to bring us home. School lasted until 3:30, so we never had to stay after school. The reason for this getting out early was because the streetcar only ran once an hour to Whitefish Bay, and it was at Oakland and Atwater at 3:30, so we had to be there or wait until 4:30. My parents wouldn't allow this, so the school had to let us out early.

My first six years of grade school were at St. Robert's Catholic school in Shorewood. I went to Whitefish Bay public school during seventh and eighth grades and graduated in 1926, then on to Shorewood High School from which I graduated in 1931. I participated in football, swimming and volleyball in high school.

While in high school, my friend Carl Birkholz and I purchased a Ford touring car, the last model that was made (1927). We started out in this Model T for the West to see the world. We left home in July 1929 and didn't return until November 1929. We learned a lot about life on this trip.

I didn't go to school that semester. After we returned, I worked in a filling station for two months and then returned to school for the second semester. This was the reason for my late graduation from high school.

We found an old truck chassis abandoned in a lot on Day Avenue. This thing had hard rubber tires on the wheels; it had a steering wheel and mechanical brakes. If it weren't for the steering wheel, it would have looked just like a wagon. The seat was just like a seat on a wagon, and so was the box. We used to ask the motorists going north on Lake Drive to tow us up the hill to the School Road, which was the dividing line between Whitefish Bay and Fox Point. We would then coast down the hill and see if we could make it to Day Avenue (almost a mile). We would repeat this procedure many times during the day. There weren't very many cars on the road in those days, so we could do this. One of us would always be the steerer of the thing—we would take turns.

Finally, the police would not allow us on the street anymore, so we took to the sidewalk. Then they said we had to get off the sidewalk, so we decided to push it over the lake bank at the end of Day Avenue. We were just about ready to shove it over when Mr. O'Connor came running out of his house and said we couldn't push it over there as it would clutter up his beach down below. We then proceeded south two blocks and decided to push it over the end of Lake View Avenue. Another man living there, I can't recall his name now but I think it was Mr. Wright, came running out and stopped us.

By this time, we were pretty teed off, so we decided to push it up to the rear of Mr. Viall's place. He lived about a block north of Day Avenue on the top of the lake bank. We said we would hurry up, and if he came out we would not stop but just keep pushing it right over the bank. Mr. Viall was on the Village Board, and he was instrumental in having the police after us to get our truck off the road and sidewalks. So we started to push the truck to the edge of the bank, and sure enough, he came running out shouting that we couldn't push that over the bank. We didn't stop but kept on going and shoved the truck over the bank. We watched it tumble end over end, going down the bank, finally coming to rest on the sandy beach below.

We all ran away shouting, "We hope you are satisfied now!" It took about two years before the iron on the truck was finally washed under the sand by the waves washing up on shore. This was all before Klode Park, life guard, etc.

As kids when we went to a show, we had to go to the Miramar Theatre on Oakland Avenue, just south of Folsom Place in the city of Milwaukee. Folsom Place was later changed to East Locust Street. At this theater, they showed the serial movie on Saturday afternoon. Such stars as Pearl White, Ruth Roland and a fellow by name of "Hurricane Hutch" were the attractions. The movies were always cliffhangers, and you would be left hanging in

The old truck chassis Sullivan and his friends drove down the Lake Drive hill might have looked something akin to the one shown here. *Whitefish Bay Historical Society.*

suspense until the next week to see how the hero or heroine would get out of a particular situation.

We boys would then try and enact some of the scenes, such as hanging over a cliff by a rope. We would act these out up at the steep lake bank, where Klode Park is now located. It was a real steep bank. In the winter, after a blizzard, the snow would harden and lap over the top of the bank. We would then sit on the edge of the protruding snow and wiggle around, and finally a big chunk of icy snow with one of us sitting on it would break off and we would have a nice ride down the steep hill or bank. It acted as a toboggan. We used to make our own fun in those days.

In the summer, we would walk up and down the beach and find washed-up boards, planks and old wood. Then [we'd] float them down to the foot of Day Avenue and nail them together and make rafts out of them. We would then go out in about six or eight feet of water and dive for stones. One of the fellows who used to do all these things with us was my friend Bill Klatte, who lived up the street from us on Day Avenue. I met Bill when we moved to Day Avenue in 1917, and we were friends over the years until he died of a heart attack in 1966 at the age of fifty-six. It was quite a shock to me, and I missed him very much for a number of years.

From Day Avenue in 1929, we moved into a new brick colonial home at 5715 North Lake Drive, which our parents had built for us. We lived there until 1937, when my folks moved to Palmyra, Wisconsin. That is the year I got married.

Besides the paper route, I had other jobs during my growing up in Whitefish Bay. I took orders for magazines for the Curtis Publishing Company. The magazines were the *Saturday Evening Post*, the *Ladies Home Journal* and the *Country Gentleman*. I had a couple of customers in the neighborhood that I took care of their lawns in the summertime and snow shoveling in the winter. Can you imagine shoveling a forty-foot lot with a full driveway and a walk all around the side of the house to the back door and out to the garage for thirty-five cents? If the snow was real deep, they would pay fifty cents. Also, they paid thirty-five cents for cutting and trimming the lawn.

Another job I had was watching the tailor shop when the owner went home for supper for about an hour and a half. I would hand out the cleaned clothes as the customers came in to pick them up. The tailor used to press the clothes by hand with a large steam iron. I used to sneak my trousers in, and while the tailor was gone, I would press them, saving myself a few cents. I also started to deliver for the drugstore on a bicycle with a bag over my shoulder. Later, as I grew older and could drive, I would deliver by car.

I also clerked in the store and worked at the soda fountain. I also worked in the Standard Oil Filling station pumping gas by hand (there were no electric pumps in those days). Saturdays and Sundays were twelve hours a day work. This was before the Wage and Hour Law came into effect.

During my high school years, I owned about seven different old Model T Fords. My first one was a roadster, which I purchased from my older brother, Robert, for thirteen dollars when I was fourteen years old. This was before they issued drivers' licenses, so nobody checked me out. I had no insurance on any of these cars. Nobody worried about that in those days because there were so few cars on the road. I shudder now when I think what could have happened to my father if I had had a serious accident. I was a minor, and they could have sued him for everything he had. The Lord was with me, I guess, because that never happened.

In the late summer of 1921, my dad, my two brothers, Herbert and Bud, and myself drove up to Iron River, Michigan. My mother's sister, our aunt Daisy, and her family were living there at the time. We made the trip in a 1912 Locomobile touring car that my dad had recently purchased. It was a large car with 37 x 5 size tires. It had straps to hold the top in place when the top was up. You could also put the top down, and then it was an open car. You only put the top up when it rained. You would also then have to snap on the side curtains to prevent the rain from coming in. These straps ran from the top of the windshield at the front of the car top, down to a place near the headlamps, where they were fastened down. It was a two-day trip at that time. Today, you can make it in a few hours. Of course, we didn't have the paved highways like we have today. In those days, there were dirt roads, and when it rained the roads became very slippery. Many times on the way up there we got stuck and would have to get a farmer to pull us out with his team of horses. We had a nice visit in Iron River and stayed a few days before returning home.

While we were there, we put the car in their garage. One day, our little cousin came running into the house and told his mother that smoke was coming out of the garage. My dad ran out to the garage and, lo and behold, the car was on fire. It started from a short in the wiring. It was lucky that Dad got there in time to put out the fire—otherwise it might have blown up, as the gas tank was black from the flames after the fire. Everything worked out okay, and we made the return trip home safely.

A couple of years later, my aunt Daisy and her family moved to Menomonee, Michigan. We again went up to visit, and this time I stayed on to visit with my cousins. Menomonee, Michigan, is just across the river

The 1912 Locomobile Touring Car was a grand vehicle. In 1912, the Locomobile 6-48, Model M, five-passenger "Sportsman" Torpedo Touring retailed for $4,800, compared to a similar Cadillac, which sold at $1,800. The average salary in 1912 was $750 a year. *Photograph courtesy of flynwheels.com.*

from Marinette, Wisconsin. My cousin Glen and I would walk across the bridge to Marinette and go through the big department store there. I think it was called "Lauerman's." We would also go swimming in Green Bay (the water, not the city). We also went with the whole family over to Hennes Park for a picnic. I had a wonderful time while there. I came back to Milwaukee on the train (my first train ride). I was really excited! It was the Chicago & Northwestern Line, and at that time, the tracks ran right through Whitefish Bay, a block from our home on Day Avenue. What a thrill to go through my own neighborhood on the train and see my home and all the other familiar sights. The train didn't stop in Whitefish Bay, so I had to ride all the way downtown to the depot on the lakefront. My dad was there to meet me and brought me home. I'll never forget that first train ride!

In the summer of 1933, while I was unemployed, there was a job opening for a few men as extras working on the railroad as section hands ("Gandyl dancers"). The pay was twenty-eight cents per hour. This was the Chicago & Northwestern Railroad right of way called the "cut-off." It ran west from Fox Point to the other Northwestern tracks, which ran northwest out of Milwaukee. These tracks joined about two or three miles west of Fox Point. Originally, this track continued out of Milwaukee northward through Shorewood Whitefish Bay and Fox Point and continued on north. However, in the early '20s, the Village Board of Whitefish Bay (my father was on the board at that time) was successful in getting the Northwestern Railroad to move their tracks out of the village. The original track formed a "Y" at about what is now East Hampton Avenue and North Marlborough Avenue, which was the southwestern corner of Whitefish Bay, and the line cut right through the village of Whitefish Bay. This was the line that was eliminated from this point to a point just west and north of the Milwaukee (Country Day School in the northwest corner of Whitefish Bay). The so-called cut-off ran from this point west where, as I said before, it joined the other track that was originally the other part of the "Y" I spoke of in the southwest part of the village.

This point of the cut-off at Fox Point is at a very high location, so in order to meet the other track two or three miles west, they had to cross some very low land. This all had to be filled in, so a wall of dirt, about twenty or thirty feet high, had to be made in order to lay the tracks on it. This dirt, or ground, came from the high spot at the start of the cut-off in Fox Point. This work was done with mule team and scoops and dumping the dirt into gondola cars. As this mound got to the right height, they would lay the track and keep going. They kept this up until they met the other track. The whole project took about two years to complete. As this was all loose dirt that built this right of way, it would keep settling. As a result, they had to keep putting stone under the track to keep it level. The trains would have to travel very slowly over this portion of the track. This took many years of doing this until the right of way finally became solid enough to sustain itself.

In order to get the stone under the track and the ties, the gang would raise the track about six inches at a time for about fifty feet. This was accomplished with large jacks. Before we raised the track, a gondola car carrying the small white stones would be brought in, and we would open the trapdoors on the floor of the cars and drop the stones onto the track a little at a time. Then, as the track was raised, a whole crew of men, probably twenty men, would join up in groups of four to a tie, two abreast on each side of a tie and facing each other. Then, using a flat-edged, short-handled shovel, we would all tamp these stones under the ties and move back and forth until the six inches we had raised were all tamped in with stone. We would continue this process up and down the cutoff until the desired height was reached. It was a real hard labor, and all this for twenty-eight cents per hour, eight hours a day. Sometimes I could have a day off, but this was during the Depression, and if you didn't want the job, there were many on the waiting list to take your place.

This work lasted all summer until the job was completed. I learned how to chew tobacco on this job, as it was the only way to keep your mouth moist and your lips from cracking from the hot, boiling sun. You know, the sun would reflect off the white stones and come right back in your face.

I met my wife-to-be, Mary, in St. Monica's Catholic Church in Whitefish Bay. I was sitting in the pew when this young lady came in with an elderly man, and they sat in the pew where I was—she sitting next to me. I had seen this girl walking down the street going to the streetcar a number of times. But now that she was seated next to me, I was determined to find out who she was and where she lived. I watched where she went after Mass, and she and this man walked to a home about a block from church. I figured this man was her father or older brother.

At this time, the village of Whitefish Bay had a directory of all residents. This was arranged not only by name but [also] by street address. The names given were Mr. & Mrs. Louis P. Kiehm, Mrs. J. Murtaugh and a Miss Mary Murtaugh. Now I had it, I knew her name and figured she was some relative of the Kiehms. That evening, I called her and told her I was the handsome young man who sat next to her in church that morning. I figured as long as we were both in church, she would think I was a pretty good OK guy (which, of course, I was). She was very evasive and didn't give me any encouragement. So, after asking if I could call again, I hung up. I didn't call her for about a month, as I worked every night in the filling station. But then, one Sunday night when I did not have to work, I decided to call her again. This time she was more friendly, and we talked for quite a while. It was then I found out why she was so abrupt and short with me the first time I called. Her boyfriend at the time was there and standing next to her while she was talking to me. Well, finally I was allowed to call on her, and we had our first date. I knew right away she was the girl for me, and I made up my mind I was going to marry her. That first date was in January 1933. This, of course, was in the midst of the Depression, and not much money was around. So, after a long courtship, we were married at St. Monica's Catholic Church on June 19, 1937. Mary Murtaugh, my wife, was born December 1, 1910, in Milwaukee, Wisconsin.

When Mary and I were married, we drove to Niagara Falls and New York City on our honeymoon. It was a great trip; we drove over the George Washington Bridge, through the Holland Tunnel and took a bus ride up through town. We went to the top of the Empire State Building. We spent our nights in New York City at the Taft Hotel. While at Niagara Falls, we took the boat ride on the *Maid-of-the-Mists* and went right under the falls and got sprayed. They furnished us with oilskin raincoats so we wouldn't get wet.

The first month of our marriage after we returned from our honeymoon, we lived at the Kiehm residence in Whitefish Bay. The Kiehms spent the entire summer at their cottage on Little Cedar Lake, which is near West Bend, Wisconsin.

Jack Sullivan died on December 24, 2004, at the age of ninety-two years—thirty-two years after writing the above narrative.

Chapter 14

GOING DOWN THE BANK

WRITTEN BY JIM HAUPT IN 1992

The author of this story starts with the following note: "This writing attempts to describe the Lake Michigan shoreline of Whitefish Bay as it existed from about 1936 to 1943. Fifty to one hundred feet of sand beach was not uncommon. Today it lies buried. Through memory, I will attempt to uncover it. Thrown in are some observations, assumptions and personal experiences that may or may not be either informative or entertaining. Because this is a unique eyewitness report, the writer is reluctant to be repudiated by other witnesses."

The high bluff along the shore of Whitefish Bay is just one block from our old family home. The bank was a forbidden place to me as a boy. Crossing Lake Drive or Silver Spring Road was the first milestone in growing up for the kids in our house. Then we had to learn to get to the stores, like the Whitefish Bay Pharmacy when Dan Fitzgerald was just the manager or Krausers IGA next door. Grandma Klann's general store and Post Office was another memory. A dangerous pastime like going down the bank was out of the question. Consequently, the area "down the bank" became the alluring, exciting playground of my youth. Its fascination has continued for over half a century.

Up at the end of our street, just north of Silver Spring, were empty lake lots. Only a few trees and an old tin garage broke the full view of the lake. It was not the usual structure one might see on North Shore Drive these days, but it became a common sight to us. That lot was fenced, and tire tracks told us it must be a garage. It was nestled tight to the brink of the bank, and close by we could see the top end of a steel stairway leading down the bank.

When the wind was off the lake, we flew kites from the lot to the north of the tin garage. Lying in the grass working the kite string I found out, from some older guys, the tin garage really belonged to the "Bootlegger." I never was quite sure what "Bootlegger" meant, but it sounded sort of scary.

At some earlier time, a piece of the bank must have slipped creating a semi-level spot halfway down. We gathered pussy willows there to sell door to door. Small bunches went for a nickel, but some nice ladies paid as much as fifteen cents. Of course, some of the evidence came home, but we explained they grew only halfway down the bank. I came home with some white trilliums just once. My mom, although appreciative, said once the flower of a trillium was picked, it never grew again.

So it was against the law to disturb a wild trillium; there were not that many trilliums anyway. Getting anymore meant crossing the Bootlegger's fence; going right past the NO TRESPASSING sign. Didn't know what "trespass" meant either, but I understood "No," and it seemed to go with "Bootlegger."

For the first couple of years, we gave the place a wide berth. Rumor was he had a gun. Once on the shore, we could see a formidable concrete fortress rising eight feet over the sand and topped with some strands of barbed wire. Front bars guarded several small windows set high in the wall, and a big boom rose over the fifty-foot-long structure. It was truly a fortress built into the teeth of the waves. The "Bootleggers" was a mystery of life. In all the time I knew of the place, I never saw the Bootlegger man, but I knew he was there—some of the time.

An easy way down to the lake was a wooden stairway at the head of Silver Spring. Wide, maybe six-foot, steps were set in series separated by even wider landings. Benches provided a resting spot and overlook; otherwise, it was a marathon climb. North was the Bootlegger's and the best sand beach on all of the bay. The slope was thickly wooded except for an unexplainable bare spot at the head of Carlisle. Down from Day Avenue was a large wooden boathouse, worn gray with weather. Some chunks of concrete lying there suggested the remains of a docking pier. (Maybe it was the Whitefish Bay Yacht Club.) Going up the hill was an old set of steps. Many owners had constructed some sort of steps for access to the beach.

Getting closer to Klode Park we saw a box-like concrete thing that appeared to be slowly sliding down the bank. It became the fort of successive neighborhood gangs. Anyway, that was "Brennan" country, and we stood clear.

Klode Park Beach was constantly being remodeled, but nothing fancier than a shack for the guard, maybe a new boat, outhouses, finally a small retaining wall. The local big guys would impress us by swimming way out and then stand up waving from an unseen but real sandbar. Some said it was really a big rock. The north end of Klode was marked by the outfall of a large-diameter storm sewer—great place for amateur spelunking. Never went in more than fifty feet myself but heard tell of others going in with ropes and lanterns. In time, a chain-link fence indicated someone wanted no traffic north. We all thought it was a transgression of our navigational rights. The beach north of Klode was big—the most protected. This is near the center or innermost part of the bay itself. The Klodes, who lived up top, had a little boathouse, as did the neighbors, and then way up north were the Fox Point Jetties—four, as I remember.

It was also the site of some lakeshore industry. Stone piles remain in eight to ten feet of water defining a pier line. Concrete stanchions there looked like anchors for rail ties. An old rusty boiler section was half buried in the sand. And it appears there is here an outcropping of ledge rock. To this day, I've never discovered the origins. Except for an occasional tramp out to Doctor's Park along the shoreline, we left the northern part of this world alone.

Whitefish Bay had (or has under water) two limestone jetties, and there were also three wooden jetties fifty years ago—but first the wall. The old seawall extended south from near Silver Spring. At that point laid the remains of an old foundation, tipped so that it looked like a huge concrete wedge—small end down and toward the water. Maybe it had been an old boathouse that upended somehow. Often the waves would wash the tip, and climbing over it, we found it hollow. Some horizontal trees and wet clay banks was evidence of a semi-active slide here. From time to time, other slides occurred. Some moved clumps of ground tied together by tree roots. They were islands in a mass of clay umber to red with varying degrees of stability. Went in to the knees more than once. The sea wall was probably designed and built to hold back the bank. The wall was concrete, a good two feet thick and five or six feet over the sand. We could walk the sand all the way to the jetties (about the south end of Circle Drive), but we also walked the wall.

At the time (pre-1940), the site of the jetties was the most popular swimming beach in the bay. Unguarded, a scramble to get to, moderately secluded, it became the place to be.

The jetties were two pier-like protrusions into the lake built to deter the lake from consuming the shore. Huge limestone slabs were evidently machine laid in courses with an overlapping bond. Roughly two-foot-thick, four-foot-wide quarry slabs were laid up eighty to one hundred feet out into the water. The two piers stood more than one hundred feet apart and sixteen to twenty inches over the water on a calm day. For the most part, the stone slabs resisted displacement of wave action

Some people caught lots of perch while sitting on that north jetty. "Frank the Fisherman" was one. He used to walk up our street, long cane poles over a shoulder, minnow bucket in his grasp and often smoking a pipe. Old Frank always had a word for us, and it was great fun to check his bucket on the way back. I think he was a carpenter; anyway, he was nice to kids.

Up on top, along Lake Drive, there were still some empty lots. One was at the north line of Lexington. A worn footpath through the grasses passed a big oak (it's still there) and led to the route down the bank where the jetties people played. [We] used to sled that path so much in the winter that it iced up like a bobsled run. The trick was to turn sharp right at the bottom to run out on the shore ice and not into the water.

At the bottom end of the path and way out in the lake there were a couple of poles sticking up, one four and the other over six feet. It became the Whitefish Bay swimming qualification test to make it to the poles without stopping; there was also a short one on the way out. Years later, I learned it was all that was left of a long docking pier for the excursion boats that serviced the Whitefish Bay Resort. That also explained the "big wall."

The big wall apparently contained the property of the resort starting just south of the jetties and continuing to Henry Clay. It existed much the way it had been built—a massive masterpiece of concrete work. At least three feet wide at the base, it stood six feet plus over the sand and was capped with a five-inch coping. Every so often, it was interrupted with six-foot-wide steps to the sand. Each set of steps was straddled by large cubic stones of concrete atop the wall. Being a goodly distance from the water, the waves would only occasionally wet the wall. It well stood the test of time.

Many, many years later (when the Coho came), the lake level was way up. The high waves stole the sand from under the wall revealing wooden piles—the very reason it had endured.

Another steep path down the bank was at Henry Clay. Down below were the wood jetties. Three (he thinks) short but wide jetties were built of cribbed timbers and filled with lake stones. For us, it was another place to swim and stuff.

Some kind of seawall existed all along what is now Palisades Road. At that time, the road was only woods that looked more like a game trail. In our minds, it was an old Indian trail that we discovered. It was cross-country bike riding at its best—great with those old balloon tires.

We ended up at Buckley Beach, where there were wooden steps similar to Silver Spring. Buckley was the other swimming beach with a lifeguard (other

A drawing by Jim Haupt, the author of this story, to illustrate the appearance of the bunker. *Whitefish Bay Historical Society.*

than Klode). At my mother's direction, I biked to Buckley to take formal swimming lessons. The class was in progress when I arrived. A couple of kids were on all fours with their heads in a bucket of water learning not to inhale face down. I already knew that and neglected to sign up. There was another big storm sewer outlet at Buckley, but as I recalled, the bore was protected with iron bars.

Before they buried the Bootlegger's place, it gave up a few more secrets. One day in early 1942, we discovered the place abandoned. The Bootlegger's usual tire tracks were grown over. We actually walked down his stairs and saw the materials chute alongside. Inside the fortress, we found two rooms for living quarters. It was a shambles. The other end looked like a shop or boat storage. Found a basket of old aluminum net floats. Sat in the man's gazebo and swapped preposterous tales trying to imagine the Bootlegger's existence and apparent demise.

When this boy was near a man, he found a person who genuinely knew the Bootlegger man. The authentic source simply said he was a fellow plumber.

Well, that might explain the elaborate but Spartan building. And maybe he liked to fish the lake. And he was evidently single, so he was drafted or joined the army when World War II broke out in 1941. And I suppose in the 1930s, "Bootlegger" was not an uncommon title—maybe shared by a good portion of the thirsty male population. And I would rather not learn anymore about it. Whatever, whomever, however—he's still the Bootlegger to me.

Chapter 15

GROWING UP ON OAKLAND AVENUE

WRITTEN FEBRUARY 28, 1981, BY CHARLES M. SCHWARZ

Dear Mrs. Bird,

I read with great interest about the researching of old homes in Whitefish Bay that you are doing.

About the year 1901, my parents purchased the first house on the left side of Oakland Avenue when entering Whitefish Bay from the south (4631 North Oakland Avenue). In other words, it was on the west side of the street. Their names were Mr. Michael and Mrs. Martha Schwarz.

My dad was previously married and had two daughters from his first wife. They were Kunigunda, the eldest, and Margaret, the youngest one. His first wife died, and then my dad married my mother, who was their hired girl. He had two sons with her, Charles Michael (that's me) and Ernest Schwarz, my brother, who was in the First World War. He was in the Thirty-second Division—the "Red Arrow" Division. He got a dose of mustard gas and never regained his health. He died at the age of twenty-two.

Getting back to the house in the Bay, before it was remodeled, it had a large round tower, and there was a beautiful porch around the south and east part of the building. For us kids, it was the most beautiful thing next to paradise that could happen to us, and the woods north of us [through] which Cumberland Boulevard runs…was beautiful. But alas, a few years later, my dad took sick. Although my mother went working, there was not enough money to save the lovely old home. I think they lost it on a delinquent $1,500 mortgage. But I will never forget the fun my brother and I had playing on the tracks of the abandoned "Dummy Line" and down a ravine to Lake Michigan.

Current view of the house at 4631 North Oakland Boulevard. *Whitefish Bay Historic Preservation Commission.*

It was about sixteen or seventeen years ago that Mr. Orville Meister, who was the chief of police then, called me and asked me if I wanted to be a school crossing guard, and I said, "Yes." And I still am, I think, the oldest guard in service at this time.

I remember going to the Old Atwater School in East Milwaukee. It was a one-room building [that] handled all the grades. A few years later, they put a partition down the middle and made two rooms out of it. The only person that I know who is still with us is Clarence Barth, retired dispatcher of Shorewood Police. Then there is the Walter Gore family, who was our closest neighbor, and the Loy family, whose home is still on the 5000 block of Santa Monica Boulevard.

Well, as of now, that is all that I can remember. If this little bit of information helps you in any way, you can use it. Otherwise, throw it away.

Sincerely Yours,
Charles M. Schwarz
Aged eighty-one years (1981)

Chapter 16

WOMAN MISSING, WHITEFISH BAY

BY ROBERT CLOVER JOHNSON

Of all the events that have occurred in Whitefish Bay over the years, this story is among the most tragic. Now, some ninety years after the incidents, the grandson of Edward Ray and Ora Belle Tompkins recites the story and provides us with a fresh perspective.

One hazy Saturday morning in October 1993, after my flight from Washington, D.C., landed at Milwaukee's General Mitchell Field, I drove a rental car to Whitefish Bay, parked on Bartlett Drive and began walking slowly toward Chateau Place, gazing at my grandfather E. Ray Tompkins' second and last completed apartment building.

Originally called "Edgewater Apartments" because he considered the structure close enough to Lake Drive and the bluffs overlooking Lake Michigan to merit that name, the building was exactly as it appeared in the 1923 newspaper halftones, except now I could appreciate the contrasting colors and textures: the raw sienna brick and tan stucco façade, the bunched rows of crisply white-sashed windows and the varied grays of the front entry with its irregular quoins, its dramatic stone arch with a shield-shaped keystone and its peaked, fully paned front door and sidelights. Beneath the stairwell windows above the front entry were two strikingly designed planters for spring and summer flowers, and higher still, surrounding a large central chimney, the building's brown-shingled, hipped roof contained two fourth-level apartments peeking out through an abundance of shed-dormer windows, some of which must have offered dramatic views of the lake. To the right of the main building was a four-

This picture, taken about 1914, shows Edward Ray Tompkins and his wife, Ora Belle (Clover), and their young daughter, Marjorie. *Robert C. Johnson.*

car garage with matching brick and an apartment on top sporting its own chimney and a bungalow-style roof.

I couldn't help feeling a certain pride in my grandfather's achievement in spite of his ultimate disgrace.

An elderly woman was walking her small white dog on the sidewalk. A jogger passed her, running east toward Lake Drive. The scene appeared completely normal, and it was astonishing to realize that seventy years earlier, when a steam shovel drove up Bartlett Drive to break ground on the vacant lot, Oswald Lupinski, a building contractor who lived in the large gambrel-roofed home across Chateau Place (then called "Luther Street"), summoned the village marshal, who arrested one of the men on the shovel. When a crowd of villagers and members of the village board convened at Village Hall, then on Fleetwood Place, for an emergency meeting, E. Ray Tompkins substituted himself for the steam shovel operator as the principal responsible party. He maintained he had a permit to build, but village officers contended the permit had been revoked due to concerns that an apartment building on Luther Street would violate recent zoning laws. Many Whitefish Bay residents said they didn't want "cliff dwellers" in their midst, a reference to the then-recent discovery of ancient adobe dwellings in Arizona with perhaps a hint of disdain for the poor inhabitants of big-city tenements. As described in the *Milwaukee Journal*:

> *The villagers turned out* en masse *to attend a session extraordinary of the village board at which the thing was threshed out. Finally, the charge was dismissed, an injunction to prevent erection of the building was dissolved, and construction continued, but the village took steps to make sure the Tompkins apartment will be lonesome in Whitefish Bay, the only one of the species extant.*[8]

Taking a look at the houses nearby, it occurred to me that the apartment building fit in about as well as any other structure in the neighborhood, which consists of an eclectic mix of Tudor, Prairie, Gambrel, Colonial and Craftsman styles, except that, being larger than the surrounding houses, it could be mistaken for someone's mansion, minus the grounds. I've been told that the building is not just accepted now but truly appreciated, partly because it is well designed and maintained and also, in part, because its unusual history gives it a certain *frisson* for those who know. After an article by Dennis McCann concerning my relationship to Ray Tompkins was published in the *Milwaukee Journal* in 1993,[9] I received letters from several people saying their hearts still beat faster whenever they walked or drove past the place. One individual, who happened to live in the garage apartment, called me on the phone and said that a kindly ghost was believed to haunt the building, sometimes quietly calling out through the heating ducts.

Beginnings

When Ray Tompkins and his partner, Phil Ebert, of the Ebert Construction Company and a team of contractors built the Edgewater Apartments, Ray was at the top of his game professionally, finally beginning to fulfill the promise suggested by his academic career. The only child of Samuel and Mary Tompkins, who owned a farm two miles south of Downs, Illinois, Ray had been quite sickly and "was not expected to live" during his earliest years. His father, Samuel Tompkins, testified in 1923 that Ray never seemed interested in playing with other children and early dedicated himself almost exclusively to academic work, at which he excelled. He was valedictorian of his graduating class in high school, of his senior class at Illinois University and Normal School (IUNS) in Normal, Illinois, and of his cohort of master's degree students at Bradley Polytechnic Institute in Peoria, Illinois.

Samuel Tompkins also said that his son "absolutely refused at any time to room with anyone."[10] This may be why Ray had to work as a "field hand"[11] at the farm after graduating from high school, while Samuel established himself as a realtor in Bloomington, Illinois, and then sold the farm and bought a house on Bell Street near the southern end of a streetcar line that ran all the way to the IUNS campus. This change of vocation and address enabled Ray to have his own room at home and commute two miles north to his classes in Normal, Illinois.

Edward Ray Tompkins. *Robert C. Johnson.*

In 1907, Ray won a competition to give the student presentation, entitled "The Triumph of Immaculate Purpose," at the fiftieth-anniversary celebration of the founding of IUNS. At Bradley Polytechnic, Ray so impressed Charles Bennett, PhD, then the world's foremost authority on manual and industrial arts training in the United States and Europe, that in 1911 Bennett advised Dr. Charles McKenna, president of the Milwaukee Normal School, that Ray was the "best man" to head the school's manual arts teacher training program. That recommendation enabled Ray and his wife, Ora, to move to Milwaukee from Grand Forks, North Dakota, in 1912.[12]

Edward Ray Tompkins met Ora Belle Clover at the Bradley Polytechnic Institute in the fall semester of 1908. The Peoria City Directory for that year lists them as boarding with landladies in houses just five doors from each other on the west side of Institute Place, a boulevard that ran north from the institute's streetcar stop on Main Street to an intersection with Columbia Terrace, which at that time featured a statue of Columbus that carriages and automobiles had to circumnavigate. Ora and Ray were two attractive adults in their twenties, of medium height, suitably dressed and satcheled for their respective academic programs. Ora probably wore a puffy-sleeved white blouse and full-length black skirt, her dark hair brushed back over her ears and tied in a bun. Ray likely wore a three-piece suit with a tall white collar and fashionably speckled tie.

Ora was an elementary school teacher in Vermillion County, Indiana, taking a year's leave to study current home economics theory and other subjects to help with her teaching. She was the second eldest of eight children of Mary Alice and William ("Billy") Clover, all of whom grew up on the Clover farm, five miles west of Clinton, Indiana, near the Illinois state line.

Ora Belle Clover as a young lady, age sixteen or seventeen. *Robert C. Johnson.*

Although her stated reason for attending Bradley made sense, there is ample reason to believe that Ora had other motives for temporarily leaving her teaching job. At the age of twenty-seven years and seven months, with a younger sister happily married and her only older sister engaged to be married the following June, she also must have been hoping to find a suitable husband at Bradley, ideally a man of ambition and vision matching her own.

As Ora and Ray got to know each other, it at some point became apparent to Ora that Ray was nearly three years her junior. Shortly before my father, Kenneth Johnson, died in 1995, he told me that my mother, Marjorie, once told him that Ora's decision not to reveal their true age difference until they were seriously considering marriage became a source of resentment for Ray that lasted throughout their entire relationship. My mother apparently never forgot hearing this grievance mentioned in arguments between her parents when she was a child.

In a letter Ray wrote to Ora in 1909 that was copied and published in 1923 in the *Milwaukee Journal*, Ray apologizes for having questioned Ora harshly during his first visit to the Clover farm in July, shortly after Ora's elder sister, Edith, married Asa Hess, a car salesman who lived in Dana, Indiana. The upset quite likely was about Ora's secrecy concerning her age. In Ray's letter, addressed to "My Dear Fiancée," Ray proposes marriage to Ora and thanks her for not reacting to his peevishness with anger. As we shall see, Ora was quite capable of anger, but in this case, she must have known that Ray was understandably hurt and bore his words with admirable restraint.[13]

They didn't marry until September 1910, partly because Ray wanted to be sure he would be allowed to continue teaching at Central High School in Grand Forks before committing himself to the marriage. Once his continuance was guaranteed, they did get married in the Clover farmhouse on September 2, 1910, with parents from both sides and a total of fifty guests in attendance, their birth dates clearly written for all to see in the Vermillion County Courthouse marriage license registry as "February 4, 1881" for Ora and "December 6, 1883" for Ray. After the ceremony, they went by train to Chicago for their honeymoon and then on to North Dakota.[14]

Ray and Ora's first child, Walter, born in their rental house in Grand Forks, quite likely with the assistance of Ora's mother, Mary Alice, died of spinal meningitis in April 1912 at the age of ten months, just as the couple was making final preparations for moving to a house near the Milwaukee Normal School in June. The boy was buried in the Tompkins family plot at Evergreen Cemetery in Bloomington, Illinois, and the many Clover and Tompkins relatives in attendance later recalled Ora saying she wished to be buried beside her firstborn son when she died. Walter was the first grandchild of both Ray's and Ora's parents. The couple arrived in Milwaukee two months later in a state of grief.

During their first two years in Milwaukee, while Ray was concentrating on developing the manual arts teacher training program at Milwaukee Normal, he and Ora quarreled often about allowing or not allowing relatives to stay with them in their half of a duplex at 856 Marietta Avenue,[15] just inside the northern border of Milwaukee. Ray said he was used to a quiet environment in which to read and think and couldn't bear the thought of a crowd of people distracting him from his work. His tendency to prefer spending his evenings studying or preparing for teaching rather than in what he saw as "this or that social function which interested me not at all" had become a source of grief for Ora.[16] After all, she had in part chosen Ray to be her husband because his projected career path suggested they would at some point be living in an interesting city like Milwaukee, a place full of potential entertainments and a likely destination point for visits by her mother, her sisters and all those kin who yearned to experience some of the pleasures and adventures of cosmopolitan living. Ray may have suggested such relatives could stay in the Pfister Hotel, to which Ora would likely have replied that her relatives couldn't afford such luxury. Ray testified tearfully in 1923 that Ora once quarreled with him because he never seemed interested in going dancing with her or doing anything for fun and that she got more benefit from Milwaukee County than from being married to him.

It was likely during this time that Ora began to collect essays, newspaper articles and quotations she copied from books in a scrapbook that she could read when other emotional support seemed lacking. Years later, the *Milwaukee Journal* described this repository as containing quotations in Ora's hand from books by Emerson, Kant, the Apostle Paul, Bishop Spalding, Oliver Wendell Holmes and many others.[17] Reading about Ora's collection eerily reminded me of my mother Marjorie's piles of consoling articles from *Reader's Digest* and other publications, which she stored in a cabinet for rereading in times of trouble, a habit she must have learned from her own mother. The *Milwaukee Journal* article notes that in her scrapbook, Ora had copied the following sentences from Emerson's essay "Friendship": "If you serve your friend because it is fit for you to serve him, do not take back your service when foolish people condemn you. Adhere to your own act." This quotation hints at why Ora remained faithful to Ray and tried to help him long after many advised her to give up on him. My mother used to tell me when I was depressed that she had read Emerson's "Self-Reliance" many times to help her cope with life's struggles.

In spite of signs of trouble ahead, the couple managed to once again start a family of their own. On October 28, 1913, my mother, Marjorie, was born in the Marietta Avenue house. My uncle Robert Clover Tompkins (my namesake) was born there on August 4, 1916. Ora's younger sister, Vida, and her husband, William C. Conrad (known to family as "Con" and to

Ora Belle Clover Tompkins in 1913 or 1914. *Robert C. Johnson.*

friends and colleagues as "Will"), moved to Shorewood from Richmond, Indiana, in 1914 after Con secured a job as head of the English Department at Milwaukee's Washington High School. Con had been head of the English Department at Richmond High School, and his teaching experience provided the easiest avenue for entry into Milwaukee, where he hoped to get a writing job at one of the city's daily papers. Con indeed got a reporting job at the *Milwaukee Journal* in 1915 and was quickly promoted to the editorial department, where he worked for the next forty-five years.[18] The couple had their first child, Evelyn, while living in a duplex at 696 Cramer Avenue on July 6, 1915. They had their second child, William (nicknamed "Billy" like his maternal grandfather), on January 8, 1919, while living at 747 Murray Avenue.[19]

Once Con and Vida arrived in Shorewood, they quickly took on the role of host and hostess for visiting family and other guests. In 1918, in fact, they invited Lucy Marie Clover, Ora's youngest sister, then twenty-three years old, to live with them in their Murray Avenue home while working in the business office at the *Milwaukee Journal*, a position Con likely helped her secure. While working for the *Journal*, Lucy met a reporter and former army lieutenant named Victor Rubin, and on December 6, 1918, they married and moved to Chicago, where Rubin worked for decades as a writer and editor for various newspapers and for the U.S. Department of Labor's National Youth Administration.

Vida and Con's hospitality, which I remember enjoying as a boy in the 1950s, both relieved and saddened Ora, who had initially hoped to play such a role herself. But at least she had friends nearby and felt freer than before to encourage Ray to follow his own ambitions and, in her words, "make something for us"[20] by exploiting his talents.

RAY, THE BUILDER

Ray decided to make use of his knowledge of current architectural design, aesthetics, mechanical drawing, materials, structural engineering, plumbing, mechanical and electrical engineering, cabinetry, joinery and the proper use of tools to build and rent living quarters of various kinds on vacant lots available in Shorewood and Whitefish Bay. His first step was to buy a lot, plan a house for it and find a contractor to work with. Phil Ebert, the eponymous head of the Ebert Construction Company, agreed to a partnership with Ray. Since Ray's father, Samuel Tompkins, had by this time become a successful realtor in Bloomington, Illinois, Ray persuaded him to loan enough money to jumpstart the enterprise.

Starting a business while holding down a steady job is difficult, but Ray's determination was as strong as might be expected from the Cicero Society orator who once spoke of the "triumph of immaculate purpose." In 1923, Samuel described Ray's routine as follows: he would rise and go to a work site early each morning, work until near the time his classes would start, walk home, eat breakfast, wash up, dress for teaching, walk up Hampshire Street to Milwaukee Normal, teach his classes, do his office hours, walk home, eat dinner, change to work clothes, walk to the house site, work until "10 or 11 at night," go home, sleep and repeat the next day. The elderly Tompkins added that Ray "made money this way, saved, reinvested in other real estate ventures, and made considerable money, but not so much money as folks say he made."[21] The newspaper stories don't indicate how many houses Ray and his partner built in this period, and I have not yet managed to track them down, but I believe all of the completed houses were in Shorewood, which suited Ray's routine as long as he lived on Marietta Avenue. He later planned many houses for various lots in Whitefish Bay, and he undoubtedly would have built them had his career proceeded without interruption.

At some point near the end of the Great War, Ray designed the first of his two completed apartment buildings. This one, a handsome nine-unit structure of eclectic design, suggests that Ray was well aware of Frank Lloyd Wright's work. The building's simple box shape and sweeping hipped roof with widely overhanging eaves may have been influenced by the Prairie-style roof and box shape of Wright's 1916 Bogk house in Milwaukee, though the details of the windows and front entry are completely different. Like the Edgewater Apartments, the staircase windows have planters, in this case five, and as in Edgewater, each apartment has an abundance of natural light. A 2013 online advertisement describes the apartments as "charming" and having "lots of windows!" The uniform stucco of the exterior walls suggests Ray was aware of Pueblo revival designs. The contrast of the pale yellow walls with the dark brown window casings, planters, brick entry arch and roof shingles is very pleasing to the eye. The style of the shed dormers of a single apartment built into the center of the roof is characteristic of dormers on Craftsman homes. As is true for most buildings constructed nearly a century ago in both Shorewood and Whitefish Bay, this one still stands and can be found at 3554 North Prospect Avenue at the intersection with East Menlo Boulevard, just two blocks from the University of Wisconsin–Milwaukee.

I believe Ray and Phil Ebert got funding in 1918 to start construction of this building in the spring of 1919. I base those dates on the fact that Ray and Ora's City Directory listing for 1920 to 1922 shifts from Marietta Avenue to the Prospect Avenue site. By the summer of 1922, when the Prospect Avenue apartments were being rented out, the Tompkins family had moved to an apartment at 533 Stratford Court, close to Vida and Con's home at 517 Stratford Court.[22] The proximity of those relatives was a particular comfort to Ora and the children.

THE GREAT INFLUENZA

This sensible-sounding narrative unfortunately took place during a disastrous period for Ora, Ray and the children. In January 1919, Ray caught what then was popularly called the "Spanish flu" but is now widely known as the Great Influenza pandemic of 1918.[23] This flu is now believed by many to have had avian origin in China but to have become a swine flu near a U.S. Army camp in Kansas as a result of swine consuming bird droppings and smoke blowing through the camp as a mound of dried pig manure was burned. There was an outbreak at that camp during a time when soldiers were being transferred all around the world, and the influenza virus became more virulent as people caught it from sneezing and coughing victims traveling from country to country. There were many cases of soldiers journeying to Europe catching the flu aboard ship before arriving at the French coast, many dying in the ship and the rest spreading the disease to the front lines. The flu was called the Spanish flu only because Spain wasn't involved in the Great War and was warning potential tourists of the outbreak while France, Germany and other European countries were silent, not wanting their enemies to know their ranks were being decimated by the disease.

Soldiers returning from Europe to Boston in October 1918 are believed to have brought the flu with them, and hundreds of hardy young men at Camp Devons died within hours or minutes after catching it. The flu quickly spread to the general population in Boston, New York, Philadelphia and Baltimore. A panicked nation began to manufacture facemasks that were widely distributed but too porous to block out the as-yet not understood viral cause of the disease. On November 11, 1918, Armistice Day, cities nationwide held parades celebrating the Allied victory in Europe, spreading the disease among the crowds. Cities like Milwaukee wisely closed movie theaters and halted other gatherings before being hit by the flu. Nonetheless, by the end of 1918, 18,339 Milwaukee residents had caught the flu, and 1,108 deaths were officially attributed to it. Of 1,636 additional deaths attributed to "pneumonia" from October through December of that year, at least half of those cases are believed to have been caused by influenza, leaving a total of 2,006 Milwaukee city residents killed by the disease in 1918 alone. These totals do not include cases in subsequent months in 1919 or cases in Milwaukee suburbs, which undoubtedly had comparable numbers of fatalities.[24] By some measures, Milwaukee was fortunate. Philadelphia, for instance, had an overall total of 12,191 deaths attributed to the flu in 1918–19.[25] Worldwide, the Great Influenza pandemic of 1918–19 killed somewhere between 50 and 100 million people, making it the deadliest plague in history.[26]

Ray may have caught the virus while doing interior cabinetry work in one of his and Phil Ebert's duplexes in Shorewood. Another worker might have brought it to the worksite. Materials for construction of the North Prospect Avenue apartment building were probably being piled up at one of Otto Schomberg's lumberyards at the time. (Schomberg, a Milwaukee lumber magnate, was one of Ray's backers in both of his apartment projects, as was Stewart Markham, a trustee at the Northwestern Mutual Life Insurance Company and son of George Markham, president of that company.)[27] Ray did not die from the flu, but his case was quite serious. When he was still contagious, he probably was taken to a hospital to protect his own family and was surrounded by sick and dying patients. As frequently happened as a result of this flu, he was unconscious for some time, his hair permanently turned white and he felt so weak after he began to recover that he gave up doing manual labor for a while. This bout of serious illness must also have reminded him of his years of being a sickly child while living with his parents on the Tompkins farm, frequently visited by doctors from Bloomington or Downs, Illinois.

It may have been during his long period of recovery that Ray began to drive his Model T up and down Milwaukee's Gold Coast suburbs with an eye for purchasing lots and developing plans for projects on those lots. It is certain that he bought the lot on the northeast corner of Bartlett Avenue and Luther Street and began planning the Edgewater Apartments. He also purchased lots near Lake Drive and Silver Spring Drive in Whitefish Bay and began planning a ten-story, eighty-unit apartment building that would overlook the lake and be near the amenities of Whitefish Bay's village center. For residents who worked in downtown Milwaukee or Menomonie Valley, he planned to create a Whitefish Bay pier outfitted with commuter speedboats. He explored locations for an airport he might build near Donges Bay in Ozaukee County, where residents of Whitefish Bay or Fox Point could park their autos and commute by plane to jobs in Chicago. And he considered buying land in the same area for a lakeside golf course similar to one he'd seen at Rye, New York, that he would surround with a colony of elite summer estates of his own design.[28] In addition to those projects and numerous house projects for Whitefish Bay, he began to plan a resort he wished to construct near Bayfield, Wisconsin, where tourists could take charter cruises to the Apostle Islands.[29]

In January 1920, a year after Ray's bout with the Great Influenza, he contracted encephalitis lethargica, a disease that many medical researchers believe was a sequela of the flu, in which the virus that became dormant in warm weather had a resurgence the following winter that focused on the brain. Ray was hospitalized and for some time was in a coma, a period in which Ora may have been told that encephalitis lethargica usually causes brain lesions that can have a range of effects. The 1990 film *Awakenings*, based on the book by Oliver Sacks, dealt with patients suffering lifelong paralysis as a consequence of this 1920 outbreak, but paralysis was just one of many possible outcomes. Considering the troubles Ora already had experienced trying to understand and accommodate Ray's complex personality, she may well have wondered what sort of husband she would be coping with when, and if, he emerged from this coma.

Ray did recover, though as a changed man. His tendency to feel that his creativity and genius were inadequately appreciated worsened. He began to complain that Ora fretted too much over his habit of buying lots with money that was due to their various creditors. He would argue that some lots had to be snapped up quickly lest their availability for his building schemes be lost. He complained that Ora was constantly meddling in his business affairs, criticizing his every decision when she should be praising him for his leadership and vision.[30] He found articles supporting this view, some emphasizing the importance of a wife's encouraging words in furthering a man's career. (One such article, later found on his desk, concerned the important role Henry Ford's wife had played in fanning the embers of his genius.)[31] In his personal testimony in 1923, Ray commented that he once found an article describing the corrosive impact of a wife's continual "nagging." He said he tried to get Ora to read it, but she "refused" to do so.

Ray had many physical complaints stemming from his illness, especially headaches, and Ora took him to several clinics in search of remedies. At doctors' urging, she left the children with Vida and Con, whereupon the couple went by train to his parents' home in Bloomington in hopes that rest in a tranquil setting would help. But Ray was reminded of the helplessness he had felt as a sickly child and began to berate his parents for having caused his problems. Ora took Ray to the Clover farm, hoping for better results, but his rudeness around her relatives forced her to bring him back to Milwaukee.

FLORENCE

After the Prospect Avenue apartments were completed and plans for future enterprises were accumulating faster than they could possibly be realized,

Ray appears to have experienced a surge of self-confidence, perhaps sensing that he was becoming a man of accomplishment rather than mere potential. He not only had "immaculate purpose," he also had the "triumph" of his first apartment building, confidence in the design of the Edgewater Apartments and the enthusiastic financial backing of Schomberg, Markham, and a new supporter, Robert Kuhnmuench, a druggist from Wauwatosa.

As Ray entered this phase of seeing himself as a "success story," it occurred to him that what had held him back for so many years were people who doubted his capabilities or saw his distaste for mere "social affairs" as a flaw rather than a sign of genius. The more he thought about this, the more he came to believe that Ora was small-minded and obsessed with petty concerns and that his parents had failed to understand him from the beginning. As these thoughts grew in his mind, he decided he needed the support of a woman more capable than Ora of appreciating his unique gifts.

Ray had taught many young women over the years, so he went to the registrar's office of the Milwaukee Normal School and reviewed the names and grades of all his former female students. Among those with high marks was Florence Witmeyer, whom he recalled as intelligent and respectful. He had taught her in 1918 before his bout with influenza. Asking other faculty about Florence, he learned she was teaching at Brown Street School, a considerable distance north of her home in South Side, but reachable for her by streetcar and a short walk.[32]

Florence K. Witmeyer. *Robert C. Johnson.*

Florence lived at 752 Mineral Street[33] with her mother, Mary; her oldest sister, Lydia, who was a teacher at the Maryland Avenue School; her next older sister, Lillie, who was an invalid; and her youngest brother, August, who was a student at Marquette University. Her father, August Witmeyer, had died in 1899 but appears to have left money to help sustain the family. Florence had three other brothers, all of whom were married and had jobs and responsibilities elsewhere. Lillie had difficulty walking and could neither read nor write. Since Mary was burdened looking after Lillie on weekdays during the school year, Lydia and Florence, the main breadwinners for this household, took turns helping Lillie on weekends. They took part-time teaching or clerking jobs during the summer but tried to spend more time with Lillie during those months, giving their mother some much-deserved free time for shopping and activities at one of South Side's many Catholic churches. Unsurprisingly, when interviewed in 1923, Florence said, "I was someone who never went out with anyone."[34]

There is some confusion as to when Ray first reacquainted himself with his former student. In her newspaper interviews, with an attorney at her side, Florence claimed that Ray appeared out of the blue at her home on Mineral Street on July 18, 1922, and offered her a job as a stenographer for Ray's correspondence work and as a helper regarding various aspects of getting approval and funding for his ten-story, eighty-unit building. The work would happen in an office Ray was renting in the Colby-Abbott Building on Water Street. She said Ray tried to talk her into giving up her teaching job to work for him year-round, promising her more money than she was earning at Brown Street School. She turned down that offer, feeling uneasy about working alone with a married man, but after Ray assured her he intended only a business association, she accepted a part-time position for the summer. She said that although her mother objected at first for the same reason Florence did, Ray won Mary over when she mentioned she had purchased some lots herself in Whitefish Bay, whereupon Ray expressed excitement and said he would gladly buy those lots from her at a good price.[35]

This story was largely true, but the meeting Florence described turned out to have occurred much earlier in 1922. After those newspaper interviews were published, police investigators found a cache of letters Florence had written to Ray, addressing him in friendly terms as early as April 1 of that year, advising him how to approach her mother when making his offer on her Whitefish Bay lots.[36] Investigators also found notes Ray had written, presumably to himself, which Ora had apparently found and transcribed in her own hand for use in the event she needed them for a lawsuit against her husband. In one of those notes, Ray stated that for Florence he had felt "love that knows no bounds though forced in secrecy for five-and-one-half years."[37]

Though I have no proof, I suspect that once Ray selected Florence as the target of his affection early in 1922, he quickly sought from her all the admiration and praise he felt he so richly deserved but could not get enough of from Ora. After all, had there truly been "love that knows no bounds" for Florence all those five and a half years, there would have been no need to review the grades of all his former female students to select her. Also, though this would not necessarily preclude an affair of the heart, from her time as a student in Milwaukee through half of 1921, Florence was living with her mother and family in Racine, Wisconsin, where she and Lydia both taught at Knapp School before the family chose to move to Milwaukee. One of the truest things Florence may have told reporters was that before Ray reappeared in her life, she hadn't thought about her former teacher at all since she attended one of his classes.

Although Florence cited July 18, 1922, as the day Ray reintroduced himself to her and met her mother, that date in reality marked the first of a series of eight mid-day meetings of Ray and Florence at various locations in Milwaukee to discuss terms of a prenuptial contract Florence would write and sign, confirming her acceptance of certain terms of marriage.[38]

Here are portions of a letter Florence mailed to Ray's business address on August 7, 1922:

> *My Dear Ray,*
> *Regarding our conferences and agreements of July 18, 19, 20, 21, 22, 23, and particularly the one at Grant Park on the 25th of July and one at Lamon Hill on the 28th, I am happy to record my agreement as follows:*
>
> *Appreciating fully the unhappy home life that has been yours and your urgent need of comfort and support as you grapple with the problems of business, I shall from now on through all the years that are to come help and sustain you in every way possible. I shall be yours and yours only, giving myself completely to you, completely and without reservation.*
>
> *...the traditional conflict between Catholic and Protestant shall not make any difference to us. We shall each maintain an open mind and strive...to appreciate the religion of the other. I will attend with you whatever church you may elect. I will permit my* [i.e. our] *children to attend your church equally as with my own and will be happy with whatever one they elect to lead their lives...*
>
> *Because of my unlimited belief that our lives will be perfectly happy I hereby agree that in the event of any failure to be so I will expect...nothing from you as a financial or property settlement. If you ask for a divorce I will grant it freely and waive all interests of a wife in your property.*

I thank you with all my heart for your suggestions of assistance for my sister and mother as well as the creation of an income for me.

It is partially in consideration of that that I waive all ordinary property rights as a wife.

I am glad we have the sources of unhappiness cleared away and the outlook is one of perfect happiness.

Florence K. Witmeyer

What follows is Ray's pledge to Florence:

My Dear Florence,

I am tremendously interested in your mother's suggestion of July 19th that you find a home in Shorewood and in your own plans "to do something" during the summer of 1922.

Let me help both you and Lydia by creating for you near Lake Drive and Newhall, Bartlett, or Oakland a double house with a three-car garage, a third apartment (small) above it.

It will be a pleasure to do it and I propose the following until the day when you are ready to fulfill your promise of July 28th, 1922.

You may then give a warranty deed in full to your mother.

Should our engagement be broken you are to deed the property wholly to me upon my payment to you of twice what you will have invested in it.

This I ask you, as you understand, because a break would make me very unhappy and your nearby residence might be a source of unhappiness, of hopes never to be realized and a source of sadness.

I will sell to you for this purpose any lots owned by me on the west side of Newhall at just what I have paid.

My compensation will be wholly in your love and companionship.

Yours forever,
E. Ray Tompkins

Buoyed by the belief that such contracts freed him from being inextricably tied to a woman with whom he later declared he had been "mismated,"[39] Ray began to idealize "Flo," as he called her, and endeavored to deepen her affection for him by giving her the rare experience of a good time. He took her riding in his Model T and showed her the completed apartment building and all the other properties he owned or hoped to own in the Milwaukee area, including the spot where he planned to build his ten-story, eighty-unit apartment building. Saying he needed her help to drum up support for a Donges Bay golf course, they played a few rounds at the Lincoln Park Golf Course in Glendale, where Ray took photos of Florence swinging a golf club for possible promotional use.[40] Not long after, Ora found some of the pictures on Ray's desk at 533 Stratford Court, and Ray didn't mind telling her about this former student who appreciated him and praised him instead of constantly criticizing him.

Alarmed by Ray's disregard for her feelings, Ora confided what seemed to be happening to her sister Vida and her brother-in-law William C. Conrad. In later testimony, Con said:

> *I went to Miss Witmeyer at the request of Mrs. Tompkins early in September, 1922, and laid before her fully the situation that had arisen because of her association with Tompkins. I pointed out to her that her rides with Tompkins into the country, her golf games with him, and their clandestine meetings were causing strife in the Tompkins household. She told me she was doing it only to help Mrs. Tompkins. I exclaimed that if she really believed that, she was pursuing a very mistaken method of assistance. I told her I brought a message from Mrs. Tompkins asking her to desist. She promised to quit seeing Tompkins, but she did not quit.*[41]

When Florence was later interviewed, she described that same meeting somewhat differently. She said that Mr. Conrad asked her if she knew she was working for "a man who is, always was, and always will be crazy" and told her to stop assisting him. She said that when she told Ray what Mr. Conrad had said, he was very angry and told her "to forget it and keep on working for him, and I did."[42]

Florence clearly enjoyed her experiences with Ray and knew how to play her part and encourage him to keep seeing her. In a letter written a few months after the photo shoots, she included the following paragraph:

> *I have found you a wonderful character in every sense of the word. Your conception of things in life has been extremely interesting to me. Your quick foresight in all things, golf, riding, etc., has proved to me that you have the ideal mind of man. With all your clean habits to help you, I should say you are a well-rounded personality worthy of great admiration. I certainly feel it is an act of Providence that I should be permitted to know such a one as you.*[43]

Increasingly confident that he could look forward to future matrimonial happiness and moral support from Florence, Ray began to feel freer to destroy what was left of his marriage to Ora.

EMERGENCY HOSPITAL

He appears to have begun to abuse her physically, perhaps for the first time, after having negotiated his prenuptial agreements with Florence in 1922. During this period, Ora began to keep a diary, probably with the intent of using her notes to document Ray's behavior in case they decided to seek a divorce. Many of the diary entries were later copied and printed in the *Milwaukee Journal*.[44] It is clear from the entries that she and her children were living with a man who was sick in mind and body. What follows are phrases or sentences as they were copied from the diary and printed in the *Journal*, with bullets added before each separate entry. The dates given are as they were used in the diary, sometimes signifying one entry only and sometimes a group of separate entries for a given period of time:

- *Can't work without inspiration. These girls give him inspiration.*
- *Wanted to draw up contracts with everybody.*
- *Always wanting me to sign certain papers.*
- *Fearful for everything.*
- *When he and God know that things are right, nothing can change him.*
- *Speaks of being lonesome.*
- *Needs someone to praise him all the time.*
- *Has wanted things quiet.*
- *Threatened me lately. Threatened to break a chair over my head. All he can do to keep from doing something to be sent to the pen.*
- *No talking or laughing at the table. "Stop that hysterical laugh."*
- *Poor judgment in business.*
- *My laundress has been afraid of him a year.*

November, 1922—

- *Was compelled to give up flat and go to Indiana with children. Could not stand the abuse of E.R.T. in my delicate condition.*

The November 1922 entry is certainly an understatement. According to a report later written by "alienists" (a term eventually superseded by "psychiatrists"), on November 6, 1922, Ray attempted to choke Ora in the kitchen of their Stratford Court apartment.[45] When she broke away from him, he proceeded to follow her out of the kitchen with a butcher knife in his hand, threatening to kill her. Eventually, he put the knife away, calmed down and went to bed. Ora, who happened to be pregnant with her and

Ray's fourth child at the time, was afraid Ray would kill her. While he was out the next morning, she went upstairs to visit B.B. Rowley, an alienist, seeking help. Rowley had heard Ray yelling at Ora many times, sometimes until two or three o'clock in the morning, and he suggested that when Ray came home from work the next evening, he and a patrolman would take Ray to Emergency Hospital in Milwaukee for "mental observation." Con, who lived a short distance away, later volunteered to go with them.

Dr. Rowley proceeded to write a petition for an examination to determine Tompkins' sanity, and he, Ora and Con all signed it. In the petition, Rowley warned hospital authorities that the man was dangerously insane and would kill his wife if released. On the evening of November 7, hoping that Ray would be committed to an institution for the insane where he would cease to be a danger to Ora or anyone else, Dr. Rowley, "Patrolman Jones" and Con compelled Ray to go for a ride in Dr. Rowley's car. At the hospital, in addition to giving the petition to the superintendent of the hospital, Dr. Rowley emphasized that Ray had a "mania to kill his wife and would do so if liberated." Ray, incensed, was left at Emergency Hospital at 9:15 that evening, where he was finally persuaded by the attending physician, a Dr. Mueller, to spend the night.[46]

Dr. Mueller later claimed that he never saw the petition and just tried to calm Ray Tompkins down and get him to bed on the assumption that specialists would examine him the next day. The hospital superintendent, Minnie Getts, later recalled that Dr. Mueller recognized Ray as one of his former professors at Milwaukee Normal School, and the two of them, surprised and excited to see each other, spoke of the normal school and never discussed the petition.[47] When he eventually heard about Ms. Getts' anecdote, Dr. Mueller disputed her story and said Tompkins had not been one of his former teachers, though he remembered seeing him occasionally on campus.[48] Ray, on the other hand, had already described Dr. Mueller as a "good friend" he had talked to at Emergency Hospital.

The next morning, Ora called Emergency Hospital to inquire about the disposition of her husband's case and was told that he had been released because he lived outside the Milwaukee city limits and therefore was not under the hospital's purview and also because it was believed that "if they held her husband in the mental observation ward he would become a raving maniac."[49]

SEPARATIONS

Knowing Ray was free to do as he chose, Ora decided to seek safety. She told Ray she was taking the children to Clinton, Indiana, to stay at the Clover farm for a while. Before she left, Ray compelled her, probably by force, to call Florence and ask her to please help her husband during her absence. Ora complied, against her will, and Florence agreed to do as Ora asked, believing Ora's request was sincere.

Sometime later in November, while Ora and the children were being looked after at the Clover farm, Ora gave birth to a stillborn baby boy. The deceased infant, named Arthur, was put in a small casket on a sideboard in the dining room for a day and then buried across what now is Route 163 in Spangler Cemetery beside Brouillette Creek. None of the articles I have read dared speculate about a possible link between the baby's death and Ray's previous abuse.

When interviewed more than a year later, Florence said that in November 1922, she was questioned by Miss Sarah Carroll, principal of Brown Street School, about her relationship with Mr. Tompkins. Milwaukee Public Schools superintendent Milton Potter had apparently expressed concern to Miss Carroll that Miss Witmeyer's relationship with Mr. Tompkins was inappropriate, and Miss Carroll apparently shared that concern. Florence said that she had insisted her relationship with Ray "was all business—there was no affection or anything like that," but Mr. Potter's and Miss Carroll's comments worried Florence enough that she decided she must end her relationship with Ray in defense of her "honor and character."[50]

After Florence explained her decision to Ray, she said:

> *He called up continually and gave me no peace...I finally acceded on the ground that his wife wanted me to help, and I went to his office Saturday afternoons and did typing for him. I went up a few evenings after school when he sent word I was needed. He called up the school, and one day he was sitting in his car when I came out. I told him he mustn't do that. It must stop. I thought of all the trouble he had brought on me and I just broke down and cried. I told him I just couldn't come and help him anymore. I told him he had a wife and beautiful children and I mustn't do anything to cause trouble. He cried too. He said, "Florence, if you can't give me some assistance, I'll have to commit murder like Professor Cheever did"—he meant murder himself, suicide—"If you can't help me, I'll kill myself some way." He simply made me feel I had to do something.*[51]

Although Ray had acknowledged to Ora that he enjoyed his association with Florence, he had also generally maintained that she was working as his stenographer at the Colby-Abbott Building and that the relationship was "proper." Perhaps as a gesture of assurance that he was not having a love affair, he found ways to include Florence in events involving Ora and the children, as if Florence was a friend of the family. His methods, however, were not delicate. In December 1923, Ora's older sister Edith described a situation she had witnessed in which Ray twisted a reluctant Ora's arm behind her back, forcing her to call Florence to invite her to Robert's sixth birthday party on August 4, 1922. Assuming Edith's testimony is valid, that was just a few days after Ray and Florence had formulated their prenuptial agreements. Odds are that the two women also met on Marjorie's birthday, on October 28, 1922. Such meetings explain why it was possible for Florence to claim that "my talking to Ray about the merits of his wife and the lovable qualities of his children is what really brought him to bring them back." Later on, there were several get-togethers including Ora, Ray, Marjorie, Robert and Florence. Florence's testimony suggests she took these to be genuinely friendly meetings, little realizing how distressed Ora was over the apparent triangulation of Ray's affections.

Also in November 1922, Carroll G. Pearse, then the president of the Milwaukee Normal School, was informed that E. Ray Tompkins had been seen playing golf and driving a car accompanied by Miss Florence Witmeyer, a teacher in Milwaukee's public school system. Pearse summoned Tompkins to explain himself. Ray spoke honestly and said he was a sick man and couldn't help himself. He requested a temporary leave of absence to seek medical help. He was granted ninety days to improve his mental and physical health and end his association with Miss Witmeyer.

During that ninety days, President Pearse resigned his position and was replaced by Frank J. Mellencamp. Ray visited President Mellencamp in January, asking to be reinstated, but after discussing the matter with the normal school's board of regents in Madison, Mellencamp decided to terminate Ray's teaching career at the school because of his "unwarranted interest in a public school teacher." Ray brought a lawyer and threatened a lawsuit but was told that there were insufficient grounds and he must seek employment elsewhere.[52] Ray was suddenly free to devote himself completely to his real estate ventures and to sorting out his personal life.

Florence retained her position at Brown Street School through the spring semester but was told that due to her continued relationship with Ray

Tompkins in spite of her superiors' concerns, she would not be retained the following year. Florence continued to work for Ray, believing Ora wished her to, but in the fall of 1923, she secured a position as clerk at a downtown Milwaukee jewelry store.

Ora, Marjorie and Robert stayed at the Clover farm through Christmas 1922. Samuel and Mary Tompkins, who had heard from her and Ray both by mail, contacted Ora and urged her and the children to stay with them for a while, in spite of whatever Ray might think. So at some point early in 1923, Ora and the children took a train to Bloomington, Illinois.

ADHERING TO HER OWN ACT

Ray began to write moody letters to his parents and to Ora, sometimes expressing anger about his humiliating experience at Emergency Hospital or about his parents having sided with the view that he was "much sick." But perhaps because of Florence's influence, he began to write conciliatory letters to Ora, encouraging her to come back. In these letters, he tried to explain the conditions in which he believed their marriage could work:

> *All that is needed or ever has been needed is for you to appreciate and recognize the fact that I am peculiar and different from most folks and then just let me go about in my own natural way and don't ever allow yourself to be influenced by gossiping, meddlesome, irresponsible, unintelligent advisers to try to warp me back into their way of looking at things...Be thankful you married the man you did, and when the snow melts away in the spring I will drive down for you and the kids in our new seven-passenger Hudson sedan. I want to doll you up. Get you a maid so you can rest and play and I want you to join the Ladies' Mite society so you won't be all loaded to talk my arm off if I come home tired and non-committal. Talk it out with the ladies: the best way to uplift the heathens in the Fiji islands. Join the society for the promotion of the production of peanuts...All you have to do to be happy is to forget responsibility and let me be the boss. If you look better to me in green shoes with square toes and a yellow hat trimmed in carmine then I think that is what you should try to find and then* [wear]. *Don't argue with me about it. Do all your arguing with the Society for the Suppression of Jazz...Wire me, kid, when you have read this as to how you feel. Yours truly, Edward Ray Tompkins*[53]

Ray's picture of a June 1923 outing with Ora, Robert and Marjorie. *Robert C. Johnson.*

Ora ultimately decided to rejoin Ray, bringing the children with her and putting them in Henry Clay School in Whitefish Bay. They moved from their Stratford Court apartment to rooms in a house on Lake Drive belonging to a Mrs. Swift and then, later, to another house on Lake Drive, both houses near the site where Ray and Phil Ebert were about to erect the second apartment building.

It was after Ora's return in April 1923 that Ray managed to successfully launch construction of the Edgewater Apartments, and in the months that followed, much of his time was spent doing manual work on the building, either supervising contractors or doing carpentry and cabinetry himself. He continued to work on plans for his ten-story, eighty-unit apartment building in Whitefish Bay and was constantly seeking bank loans (frequently rejected) to pay for lots, often while delaying payments to creditors.

Soon after Ora, Ray and the children were living together, Ray began to complain about his health, and Ora was involved in making appointments and going with him to doctors. He moaned in the night and would ask Ora to call doctors at all hours. They went to clinics, where Ray was advised that many of his physical complaints were all in his mind. At some point, Samuel and Mary Tompkins appear to have visited. Here are a few of Ora's diary entries:

May, 1923

- *Worried about appendicitis. Wrote to Drs. Dewey & Studley*
- *Had no appendicitis.*
- *Talked about it for days as if it were a fact.*
- *Then decided he had heart trouble. Went to Dr. Nelherder.*
- *"You are unduly worried about something that doesn't exist."*
- *Was antagonistic toward father, then mother, then me. Could not be in harmony with us all three at once.*

- *Didn't sleep, would lie in bed in mornings and talk by the hour.*
- *Father told him if he hunts happiness as he did trouble, he could find it.*
- *He told Ray that there wasn't one woman in a million who would live with him through his illness from the way he talked.*
- *Last fall he thought only of himself. He wouldn't take me anywhere.*
- *Puts someone between us and expected me to be happy.*

Ora and Ray went to a lawyer to apply for a divorce, but Ray had heard that in Racine they could get a divorce quietly and wouldn't even have to tell their relatives. Gradually, violence became a more frequent part of her diary entries:

> *June 14:* [Ray] *said he was going to hell and the building was going into the lake. He said he would murder me if I ever did anything in regard to his girlfriend. He grabbed me and shook me. Taunted me all morning about not wanting a divorce. I told him I was going down in the afternoon, which I did. Then I was reprimanded and abused for going to a lawyer to make application for a divorce. He wanted me to go to his lawyer. He said he was broken. He would have to get the Humane society to come and take care of him, or turn himself over to the district attorney. Then he came to our bedroom and shook and beat me, said he could murder me for not doing what he told me to do. The children and I finally got him quieted and to bed.*
> *July 3: He petted me and loved me, then told me very calmly that if it weren't for the children, he would murder me.*
> *July 4: Struck me in the back of the head with his fist. Talked ugly and hateful all day.*
> *July 5: Called me upstairs three times while I was getting breakfast. Told me then to get downstairs or he would kick me down. Wanted me to get girl in our home. Wanted me to let him get divorce. Worried me all day and half of the night.*
> *July 6–7: Was normal peaceable this morning. Everything lovely until he awoke at 4 o'clock in the morning of July 7. Talked quietly for 30 minutes then became violent. Called me to his room, when I could not stand his talk any longer and tried to leave the room, he threw me half way across the room and hurt my arm and hips. Marjorie screamed and ran downstairs and he quieted down. Went off Saturday forenoon and came home. Went to work at apartment and lawn in the afternoon. Said we would go to Racine and get divorce quietly and let no one know it, not even our parents.*

July 29: Ray went to town after lunch. Came home at 5. It is a dark future to think that we can't go anywhere or see anyone and yet he goes and sees whom he pleases at all times.
August 4: Had a party for Robert. F.W. came to it.

Sometime in September, the four-car garage with an apartment on top was completed, and Ray, Ora, Marjorie and Robert moved from their rental house on Lake Drive to this apartment. One evening, Ray and Ora drove out on Loomis Road south of Milwaukee in search of small trees to dig up and take back in the Hudson sedan to plant around the apartment.

Sept. 26: Took me out on Loomis Rd and dug a grave for me. Tried to get me to go back where he was digging. I went far enough to see that he was terribly unnatural about the whole thing. His face was gray, his lips purple and he was trembling terribly.
Sept. 28: Almost choked me to death.

In their discussions with lawyers about getting a divorce, one of the difficult and unresolved issues was what percentage of the couple's collective interest rights each would settle for.

Nov. 19: Began to talk insulting. Kept on until he became violent. Wanted me to say what I would take in settlement. I told him a one third interest. He shut Marjorie in the bedroom. I saw he was going to do me bodily harm and [started to run] *downstairs in night dress. He grabbed me when I got to top of stairs and choked me. I screamed. And so did Robert. He let loose and Robert and I ran in bedroom and locked door…Came in next morning and again used violence. Marjorie and I ran over into apartment building.*

FURY

Late one afternoon on November 28, 1923—the day before Thanksgiving—Ray called Florence at the jewelry store where she was working and asked to meet her at the Pabst Theater after she got off work. Florence later claimed that she told him she was planning to go home for dinner then but that Ray said he would kill himself if she didn't meet him, so they agreed to meet at the Pabst Theater and eat somewhere nearby.

Her story was that after dinner Ray said he wanted her to come see the last unoccupied flat at Edgewater because he had just finished working on it and wanted her to see it before a tenant moved in. Florence claimed that she had protested it would be wrong to go with Ray to an apartment in the dark but that Ray had been insistent, saying he would just show her the place for a minute and then take her home.[54]

Her story and Ora's story agree only in that Ray then drove Florence to the Edgewater Apartments, where he parked his new 1923 Ford touring car in a parking area behind the building, not in the garage.

Ora had noticed that her husband was spending most of that afternoon straightening up the apartment to which he had been banished because of his violence. She had wondered if he was expecting company. She and the children, who were in the garage apartment, may have been playing with Sporty, their white cat, or rolling out dough for a pie to take to Vida and Con's for Thanksgiving dinner the next day, but Ora heard the car engine and looked out the bedroom window to see if it might be Ray. She could see Ray walking from the car toward the back of the building, signaling all clear, and Florence getting out of the car and following. Ora apparently could see the windows of the apartment Ray had been sleeping in and saw that no lights were turned on for several minutes.[55]

She called Con on the phone and asked him to send the John T. Sullivan detectives Con and Vida had hired in case such an event occurred. Some thirty minutes later, detectives arrived. Ora showed them the apartment, which was then raided. Ray and Flo were undressed and in a "compromising position" on the Murphy bed. A photographer took pictures. Ray and Florence were compelled to sign documents admitting to adultery. Ray was additionally compelled to sign another document, which read:

> *I hereby give to my wife all my personal and real estate property, including all my holdings in the Edgewater apartment and 10½ lots in Whitefish Bay.*
>
> *E. Ray Tompkins* [signature]
> *Witnesses: John T. Sullivan and Walter Danischewsky* [signatures]

Florence later insisted that the entire event was a "frame-up" in which she was the innocent dupe of Ray and Ora, who were trying to establish grounds for their mutually desired divorce. She asserted that Ray had forcibly taken her clothing off in order to create a scene Ora and Ray had planned together. It was then pointed out that her clothing was neatly folded on a chair at the time of the raid. Also, evidence of Florence agreeing to eventually marry Ray would later cast doubt on her claims of innocence.

It may be that Ray alone planned the event, knowing detectives would likely be summoned and knowing their pictures and his signed admission would provide grounds for divorce. He probably assumed that the settlement terms could still be negotiated and that Ora would settle for only a modest percent of their property.

Somehow Florence got home that night, and somehow the Tompkins family must have gotten some sleep. Ray must have driven the family in the Ford touring car from the Edgewater Apartments to Vida and Con's Stratford Court home in Shorewood for Thanksgiving dinner. Incredible as it may seem, Ray appears to have taken his camera to this event, where he took a picture of many family members around the dining table after dessert had been eaten. Lucy Rubin is present, apparently having come up from Chicago for this special day of family togetherness. It is a dismal scene. Everyone has either heard about the scandalous event of the previous evening or is reacting to the frozen moods of the adults. Assuming Con and Lucy's husband, Victor, were there, they clearly removed themselves from inclusion in

Ray's picture of the 1923 Thanksgiving family gathering at the Conrads' house: Robert and Ora Tompkins on the left, Evelyn Conrad, Marjorie Tompkins and Lucy Rubin in the middle and Vida Conrad on the right. Ora is holding Lucy's youngest child, Lucille, in her lap. Lucy is holding her middle child, Dorothy, and Vida is holding her son Billy. Only Robert is looking toward the photographer, and his expression suggests wariness. *Robert C. Johnson.*

the picture. Most are carefully averting their gaze, but my uncle Robert, then age seven, who had often stood between his scuffling parents, pushing them apart, is glaring with obvious venom at the cameraman, his father.

There was another vacant apartment in the building, and Ora and the children moved there on Thanksgiving Day after returning from the Conrads' house. Simultaneously, Ray moved back into the well-furnished garage apartment. On December 5, Ora wrote a letter to Ray's parents[56] describing her situation:

> *Dear Father and Mother,*
> *The children and I moved into the northwest corner apartment last Thursday. We are comfortably settled and I think safe here. Ray is in the garage apt.*
>
> *Last Wednesday night a couple of detectives made a raid on this apartment where he was then sleeping and caught him and Miss Wit. in bed. Now I am going to get a settlement out of him out of court I think. That will prevent any scandal for the children to live down.*
>
> *I am going to ask for* [the] *building to be put in corporation, giving me two-thirds stock and him one third. That leaves control with me. He has offered me $20,000 third mortgage, but that would leave him the rents to handle and he might use them instead of paying on the building.*
>
> *Now* [if] *grandpa* [Samuel] *was here I would choose him for the third director, but I have to have someone who can meet with us.*
>
> *They signed a confession and Ray also turned all his holdings over to me. But I am not going to be niggardly like he has been to us. I am going to give him one third, one third to me, and hold the other third for the children. Then I'll leave him four free lots on which he may build if he wishes.*
>
> *We will draw this up tomorrow. If he balks, I will sue on grounds of adultery and I fear he will go to Waupun* [location of state prison] *and her too.*
>
> *She gets what is coming to her when I am settled up with Ray.*
>
> *They promised never to see each other again that night and it wasn't two days until they met.*
>
> *He has given up the room down town* [in Colby-Abbott Building] *and brought his rug home. Think of bringing her out here with the children and I in calling distance. Now you and father come to see us just whenever you want to. He has nothing to say about it now. We haven't lived together for a month and he has no key to this door. I never saw anyone so set on their own destruction as he is.*

He got a new Ford the other day. It doesn't do the children and I any good. Maybe some time we will have one of our own.

If things get too tense I might send for grandpa; could he come or does he want to? I have no telephone, but Vida's telephone is Edgewater 2944W.

Now the next month will decide many things. There will be some debts besides the two mortgages but by careful planning we ought to pull through.

If he would stop getting peeved at every little thing and settle down to work he could accomplish so much. The building is a fine one, but I am not going to let so low down a woman have a chance to get it away from my children. He doesn't seem to realize what a serious thing he had done. Now still send my letters to Vida's. I'll let you know how we are progressing in a few days. He doesn't know but what you folks and my people hired the detectives and they really did.

ORA

After preparing the letter for mailing at the post office the next morning, Ora put it in her handbag, which was hanging by its strap from a linen closet doorknob. Then she left the children alone in the apartment and went out to Luther Street, where Con picked her up and took her for a short visit with Vida.

Ray and Ora were planning to meet with a lawyer the next afternoon to discuss the terms of their divorce. Curious to know what percent of property interest Ora was willing to settle for, Ray went to her apartment to see if she had decided. After knocking and saying who he was, one of the children said their mother was out. Ray said he wanted to come in. The child apparently opened the door, which I assume was locked. Ray later said that for no reason he could explain, his eyes immediately lighted on the handbag. He crossed the room and, seeing that there was a letter from Ora to his parents there, he took the letter, left his children, went back to the garage apartment, tore open the envelope and read what Ora had written.

Prior to the raid on Ray and Florence, Ray and Ora had drawn up an agreement with their attorney that Ray would give Ora $156 a month until he accumulated a lump sum payment to her of $20,000, but he would retain control over their properties. In spite of the raid, Ray was hoping that those terms would be in effect. He assumed that the lasting effect of the raid was to establish grounds for divorce, not the final terms of the settlement. But Ora's letter to his own parents, saying she would have control of two-thirds of all their property and wished his father could be a one-third partner, infuriated him. The statement that as a result of his and Florence's adultery they could both go to the penitentiary enraged him. When he saw Ora returning, he confronted her in the hallway. They quarreled bitterly but briefly and agreed to talk more the next morning. Ray tossed all night, unable to sleep.

Over the course of several days, in testimony to District Attorney Shaughnessy and in a private interview with *Milwaukee Journal* writer Harry Zander,[57] Ray himself described what happened the next morning as well as anyone ever has. Here is a sequential compilation of his statements:

> *Thursday morning, the children had gone to school. I had calmed myself considerably. At 10:30 I went to her apartment with the most peaceful intentions in the world. I went to beseech her, to implore her, to live up to our earlier agreement of $156 per month and $20,000 agreed to in the lawyer's office.*
>
> *I sat on the davenport, she on a chair in front of me. I offered her $20,000 if she would go away and stay away forever. She said she might go to California. I promised I would buy her a fine home there if she would go there and stay.*
>
> *I then asked her to stop persecuting Miss Witmeyer. This triggered her fury.*
>
> *She flared up then and threatened to send me to Waupun if I didn't accede to her demands.*
>
> *She jeered at me, jibed at me. She said, "You are a fool. You can be the janitor of the apartments and live over the garage. You can scrub the hallways and take care of the furnace room. I'll buy you what you need and take care of you."*
>
> *Consider what I have done in erecting an apartment building in Shorewood and another in Whitefish Bay, all from a capital of $2,400 in a few years. Am I to be called a fool? Am I to be told I have no sense; that I can be the janitor, without rebelling? Of course I became angry.*
>
> *She reached around back of the door and got a piece of gas pipe that she had standing there and she brandished it before me as she continued to taunt and threaten me.*
>
> *I leaped. I seized her by the throat in a frenzy of rage and choked her. I squeezed as hard as I could. I held her like that for about 10 minutes. She was gasping and struggling. Then I saw that she was dead. I did not intend to kill her, so help me God. But after I had held her for a time and her struggles ceased, I saw that she was dead.*
>
> *Panic seized me! Such a terrible panic! I know now that what I should have done then was to have called the sheriff immediately and have had him come out and see what I had done. But the panic gripped me. Something seemed to tell me that I had to destroy the evidence. I seemed to move*

automatically. I have no doubt I was stark insane at that time, for I can look back and see myself moving about hurriedly there as though it was some horrible nightmare.

Then I carried her into the bathroom and, putting the body over the edge of the bathtub, I took a bone-handled knife with which she had been peeling potatoes at the sink and cut her head from the body. I turned the water on so that it would wash away the blood. I decided quickly that I would have to sever the head to prevent the body from being recognized. I rushed downstairs with the head to the furnace room and, opening the door of the furnace, I threw the head in. Then I went up and took the clothes off the torso and, returning, burned them. I wrapped the body in a blanket then and carried it out to the garage, where I put it in a trunk, out of which I had hastily dumped the contents in the basement.

I should interject that two separate accounts I have heard contradict that my grandfather carried the blanket-wrapped body outside to the garage. Journalist Arthur Tiller of Shorewood told me in 1993 that an electrician working on telephone lines outside the building watched Ray drag the trunk from the rear exit of the building to his Ford touring car and drive away. In the next chapter in this volume, Melvin Immekus provides yet another version of the story. I believe some combination of those versions is more reliable than Ray's in this instance.

Ray's confession continues:

I put the trunk with the body in it into the back of the automobile and drove out on Highway 17. It was between noon and 1 o'clock that I got to the Lion's Den [part of Jac Donges' property where Ray hoped to create either a golf course or an airport]. *My wife and my two children and I had a little picnic party out there one Sunday last June and I remembered the place as a spot of beauty.*

Leaving the garage, I had thrown a posthole spade into the automobile with which to dig the grave. Having dug the grave, I placed the body in and covered it up again. I put the trunk back in the auto and drove home. I took the trunk to the furnace room, broke it up and burned it.

Ray then hastily cleaned up Ora's apartment, bathed and changed clothes, cleaned up the Ford touring car as best he could, drove to Henry Clay School (now enlarged to be Whitefish Bay Middle School) and waited for the school session to end.

A few days later, my mother, Marjorie, age ten, was interviewed by a *Milwaukee Sentinel* writer about the rest of that day and night.[58] The interviewer described her as "a pale little figure in a black velvet dress, who sat with hands tightly clasped, puzzling aloud on the peculiarity of her father's actions Thursday afternoon…"

The children were expecting to walk home to their mother's apartment, but Ray met them on the edge of the playground and told them to get in the car. He told them he was taking them downtown for dinner. "When we asked him if he didn't want mother to come," Marjorie reported, "he just laughed and told us not to worry about mother. All the way downtown to supper, he kept joking and singing gay songs to entertain Robert and me."

Although Marjorie was terrified by the "awful suspicions" she had as a result of her father's "happy" mood, the children ate dinner as best they could in a restaurant with him then went to a toy store, where Ray insisted they pick out some toys they might like as Christmas presents. Neither child felt like picking out toys but complied to placate their father. When they got back to the apartment building and could not find Ora in her apartment, Ray told them not to worry and to stay with him that night over the garage.

Although Robert fell asleep that night, Marjorie couldn't. The reporter continues:

> *For more than a year her mother had been terrified at the very presence of her father, the child revealed, and had pleaded with the child not to leave her alone in the house with him. According to Mrs. Conrad, the sister of the murdered woman, Mrs. Tompkins had been on her guard constantly, afraid to enter a room which had a key in the door lest her husband might attack her.*
>
> *"I couldn't help knowing about it for I used to hear father threaten mother week after week and many times he struck her until I shouted that I would call the neighbors," the girl said. "But mother never let me call help or tell anyone. The only thing Robert and I could do was to stay with her and help protect her, but even that did not do much good toward the last."*
>
> *"And that was why I was so worried Thursday night when mother didn't come home," the child concluded simply. "I would have felt safer if father had tried to find her, but he wouldn't even let me call Auntie. It didn't seem natural. Then I went to bed and all the fears of the last year and all of mother's worries seemed to crowd into my throat and choke me so that I couldn't sleep."*

The next morning, when Ray stepped out of the garage apartment to talk to one of the contractors, Marjorie rushed to the telephone and called her aunt Vida to ask if her mother was there. Vida said she wasn't and that Con would drive over to get the children right away.[59] Fearing her father would block them on the stairway, Marjorie opened a window onto the garage roof. She and Robert crawled out, shut the window behind them, grabbed the gutter, then slid off the roof, dropped to the ground and waited beside Luther Street for their uncle Con.

Once Con and Vida heard the children's story, Con called Sheriff Westfahl, who, along with deputies, visited Ray Tompkins, who claimed his wife was "missing" and he had no idea where she was.

When "missing" reports appeared in the *Milwaukee Journal* and *Milwaukee Sentinel* on Friday, December 7, Jac Donges and his wife both recalled Ray Tompkins driving up in his Ford touring car shortly after noon on Thursday to ask if he could examine an area lightly covered with second-growth birch and elm and some scattered shrubs that Donges called the "Lion's Den." Ray had said he wanted to examine the land once again for possible use as a golf course. Donges had given permission and thought little of the incident until seeing the notice in the paper. He called Sheriff Westfahl that evening.[60]

Ray was being held in custody during the initial phase of the investigation into his wife's disappearance. The call from Jac Donges prompted the sheriff to examine Ray's Ford. The rubber mat in the car had a dark stain that turned out to be blood. There were scratches on the backseat and stains on the upholstery. It seems likely to me that my mother, Marjorie, may have noticed and been alarmed by some of this evidence, whether or not she told police. At the garage apartment where Ray had been living, bloodstained trousers were found.

Ray was taken to the Lion's Den early Saturday morning. Tire tracks matching the pattern of his Ford were found in the dirt road. Reporters and police together, with Ray watching, walked among the shrubs in a ravine, searching for signs of a burial. A police reporter, noticing a twig sticking out of a mound of earth, pulled on it and, along with a plug of dirt, a human hand popped out. Ray was asked to help police pull earth away from the form hidden beneath it. As Ray scraped dirt off the body, Deputy Sheriff Henry Bender commented, "A fine Christmas present you have uncovered for your two children!"

Ray, stunned, was led away for a while and then brought back to see the nude, headless body, whereupon he said, "Who could have done this thing? Find the guilty one!"

It wasn't long before Ray, the guilty one, was brought before District Attorney Shaughnessy, who allowed Ray to tell his life story, including his many accomplishments, before being coaxed into a simple confession of having strangled and beheaded his wife.

AFTERWARD

For three weeks, the Milwaukee newspapers went mad. The *Milwaukee Journal*'s first headline was "CONFESSES MURDER OF HIS WIFE; CHOKES VICTIM, CUTS OFF HEAD." The *Milwaukee Sentinel* followed with "TOMPKINS ADMITS SLAYING; Wife's Headless Body Found on Farm; WEALTHY LAND MAN BARES GUILT AFTER PLEADING INNOCENCE." The story had all the ingredients of what journalist Russell Baker, in his book *The Good Times*, calls a "terrific murder":

> *Such murders featured dismembered corpses, "statuesque" women found dead in full nudity, husbands willing to kill to inherit a rich wife's fortune or to replace a cool wife with a warm mistress, and similar elements beloved by connoisseurs of barbershop magazines like* The Police Gazette *and* True Detective. *The "terrific murder" was so rare that as a police reporter I never had the pleasure of covering one.*[61]

When Ora's diary was found and printed in the newspaper, Ray read it in jail and wept, saying he wished he had found that document in her apartment instead of the letter to his parents. He said he had come to see only Ora's combative side and had responded in kind, but after reading the diary, he told Harry Zander that "there she was, broken in nerves, in spirit, sick, needing help and love and kindness and I did not give it to her because I did not understand...Why couldn't I have found that diary instead of the letter the day before it all happened? This could never have happened then! Why did the fates twist things thus?"[62]

Florence Witmeyer was arrested on conspiracy charges but released on $500 bail, with the threat of a trial in January. Ultimately, her case was dismissed on the grounds that she was innocent of murder, and her public embarrassment was sufficient punishment for contributing to strife in Ray and Ora's marriage.

After reading about Ora's murder, more than one thousand people visited the Edgewater Apartments to see the scene of the crime. Some ventured into the basement to see the furnace.[63]

Due to popular demand, Ora's headless body was displayed for a day in the Milwaukee city morgue. Four thousand people lined up to take a look.[64]

Dr. Mueller was temporarily blamed for allowing Ray Tompkins to be released from Emergency Hospital in 1922, but ultimately no one was charged for the release. There were serious discussions in the press and in the mental health profession about taking petitions for mental evaluation of abusive spouses more seriously.[65]

After articles were published describing Ray's many threats against and abuses of Ora, twenty-two women in Milwaukee went to the district attorney's office seeking protection, "declaring that their husbands had threatened to give them the same treatment that Tompkins gave his wife."[66] One man had gotten drunk and chased his wife around the kitchen with a butcher knife in imitation of Ray. Luckily, the woman was not killed.[67]

A panel of five alienists concluded that Edward Ray Tompkins was insane when he murdered his wife. They decided that he should be committed to the Wisconsin Institution for the Criminally Insane in Waupun. District Attorney Shaughnessy commented unofficially that this was "the best that can be done to take the sting out of this as much as possible for those poor little children."[68]

Marjorie and Robert were allowed to visit Ray briefly in jail before he was sent to Waupun. Ray seems to have genuinely loved his children and had begged to see them. Robert handed Ray a picture of a Christmas tree he had drawn. Marjorie gave him a short letter she had written: "Dear Daddy, Robert would like to see you very much. So would I. What have you been wanting for a Christmas present? I hope you are all right. We are fine." She signed off with "Love, Marjorie." Ray asked how their cat Sporty was and was glad to know he, too, was "fine."[69]

Mobs gathered at the Waupun railroad station, assuming Ray would be taken to Waupun by train. But they were disappointed.[70] He was taken in a car with Sheriff Westfahl, deputies, a young offender going to the state prison in Waupun and some journalists, including Harry R. Zander. Ray spoke of his plan to be an exemplary inmate and to help others at the Institution for the Criminally Insane by setting a good example. He expressed confidence that he would eventually be set free and asked the journalists to come back to Waupun when he would be released. He looked out a window at a cloud passing over the sun and commented, "Zander, see that sun. The sun will always come out. The clouds can't last forever."[71]

Marjorie and Robert were adopted by their aunt Edith and uncle Asa, who lived in Dana, Indiana, ten miles from the Clover farm, where some of their cousins, aunts, uncles and their maternal grandparents lived. After the children arrived in Dana, it was agreed among all the elders in the family that neither Ora's nor Ray's name would ever be spoken again unless in a whisper to another elder. The young cousins of Marjorie and Robert were told never to mention or ask about their parents. Asa Hess had a Milwaukee studio shot of Marjorie and Robert printed in the *Daily Clintonian* in nearby Clinton, Indiana, with the following caption: "Marjorie and Robert Tompkins, now living with their Aunt Edith and Uncle Asa Hess in Dana, neither speak nor think about their parents anymore." All the adults in Vermillion County knew instinctively that they must act as if the children's Milwaukee County past did not exist. Even children who were not relatives appear to have learned somehow that they must never ask. One of my mother's Dana schoolmates, Marvin Carmack, a lifelong friend of Marjorie who competed with her in statewide Latin contests in high school and later became a chemistry professor at Indiana University, told me before he died that he knew nothing about his early intellectual rival's experiences in Wisconsin. When I offered to say something about those years, he waved his hand with a firm "No!"—preserving to the end his innocence of whatever trouble had occurred.

Robert Clover Tompkins excelled in schoolwork in Indiana, was a whiz at math, learned to fly airplanes in the 1930s, joined the Army Air Corps in 1942 and married his high school sweetheart, Jane Robertson, at his training base in California in June 1943. His P-38 disappeared off the toe of Italy in August of that year after his squadron successfully strafed German military equipment on the ground. Jane and my mother were both notified that he was "Missing in Action" and held out hope he would be found alive until notified that he was officially presumed to have been "Killed in Action." His remains have not been found to this day.

My mother's grades in high school were so good that she was offered a scholarship to attend Indiana University in Bloomington, Indiana. On the letter offering her this scholarship, she wrote before her death that one of her greatest regrets was that her foster parents' incomes were insufficient to allow her to accept the award. Instead, she attended Indiana State Teacher's College in Terre Haute, Indiana, taught elementary school, became a secretary in Terre Haute, met Kenneth Johnson while participating in an amateur theatrical production in that city, and became Marjorie T. Johnson on September 1, 1939, the same day Germany invaded Poland. My brother Scott was born on March 15, 1941, and I was born on February 14, 1945.

When I was eight years old, living in Pensacola, Florida, where my father worked at a synthetic fiber plant, my mother received a letter from E. Ray

Tompkins saying he would be released soon from his long confinement and planned to visit us in Pensacola. She was so shocked she fell backward onto a hard chair, clutching her forehead. A few weeks later, she got a phone call from Central State Hospital saying that her father had died of congestive heart failure. She went away for a couple of weeks to attend his funeral in Waupun and take care of various things. She later told Scott that she was impressed by how handsome her father had looked in his casket. Near the end of her journey, she attended a graveside service at Evergreen Cemetery in Bloomington, Illinois, where "Edward R. Tompkins, 1883–1954" was buried beside his first child, "Walter E. Tompkins, 1911–1912," and near a tombstone for both Samuel and Mary Tompkins. On the other side of Walter's grave marker was a tombstone for "Ora B. Tompkins, 1881–1923," where the ashes of Ora Belle's beheaded and cremated body had been buried in 1923.

My mother died of cancer in Annandale, Virginia, in 1973. In accordance with her wishes, she was cremated, and her ashes were strewn on the Potomac River.

Edgewater Apartments on East Chateau Place, Whitefish Bay. *Whitefish Bay Historic Preservation Commission.*

1923 Murder Remains Whitefish Bay's Most Gruesome

"The brilliant but erratic mind of E. Ray Tompkins, perpetrator of one of Milwaukee's ghastliest murders, still seethes restlessly in the hope he will soon be coming home." So starts a December 26, 1947 article in the *Milwaukee Sentinel* entitled "Berserk Slayer Again Makes Freedom Bid."

Editor's note: Violent crime in Whitefish Bay is extremely rare—then as well as today. The horrific nature of this murder created a sensation throughout the Milwaukee area and was also picked up by the national press. This appears to have been the only murder in the history of the village. It is included in this book to help tell the complete story of the community.

Chapter 17

THE AUGUST BAUCH FARMHOUSE

Based on an Interview with Melvin Immekus

Mr. Melvin Immekus grew up in the home next door to the one he has lived in with his wife. His parents' and grandparents' home, and the one in which his sister Vera Immekus Lawrence now lives, is at 5007 North Idlewild Avenue, [historically referred to as] the August Bauch farmhouse.

The Bauch farmhouse, in which Melvin grew up with his sister, mother and stepfather, was moved from its original location about forty-eight feet to the west, where it is now located. It was moved about 1922, when Idlewild Avenue was put through. The original fieldstone foundation was left behind, and when Mr. Immekus built his home, directly north of 5007 North Idlewild, his driveway went over the remnants of this fieldstone. He said that accounts for parts of the driveway sinking over the years. After the brick house was moved, an addition was put on it, and the side of the home became the new front of the house. A new doorway was put in, along with windows. The original front of the home, with a porch, now faces south and is a side-door entrance.

To get to school, [Melvin] would crawl through Kryzsch's dairy farm's barbed-wire fence, in their cow pasture, as a shortcut. (Kryzsch's farm was an eighty-acre farm between St. Monica and present Idlewild Avenue, Henry Clay to Silver Spring Drive.) It was the former William Swain farm.

Mr. Immekus remembers digging his parents' field by hand and planting enough potatoes to last them all winter. Then he had to look under the leaves, pick off the potato bugs, put them in a can and pour kerosene on them to kill them. He said it took a long time to look under all those leaves and get the bugs.

The Bauch farmhouse, now located at 5007 North Idlewild Avenue. This photograph was taken in 1909 and shows Frank and Caroline Christi Stahl and their son, George. The house was moved forty-eight feet to its present location in 1926. *Whitefish Bay Historical Society.*

Mr. Immekus finished a course at the Milwaukee School of Engineering, and when the Village of Whitefish Bay advertised for a mechanical engineer, he took the village test with thirty other men. He was the only one to pass the test and was hired.

In a wide-ranging interview, Mr. Immekus mentioned a house named Bella Vista and the "Kentucky Colonel" who lived in it. (This was A.F. Nussbaumer's home, on the triangle of Lake Drive, Fairmount Avenue and Bartlett Avenue—gone now.) The man was James Haynes, so named due to his white mustache and goatee. Behind his house there was a bowling alley and a pit, in which he held dog fights with pit bulls. He also held rat fights with rat terriers there. It was all illegal, but he was never arrested.

He noted A.J. Crofts had a "blind pig"[72] on the grounds of his house, located on the west side of old Lake Drive (Lake Drive was then more to the east of where it is now), just north of Henry Clay Street.

Melvin remembered that Herman Fritzke bought Croft's Saloon in 1919, tore it apart and rebuilt it with his wife, on its present site, 5128 North Idlewild Avenue. This house had been purchased by Dr. T.W. Williams and moved from the resort grounds to Kimbark Place and Lexington Boulevard. It was there when Fritzke bought it.

The Rothgens lived at 5135 North Hollywood Avenue before they built their house on the west side of Lydell Avenue, north side of Silver Spring. Their son was called "the Professor" by everyone in the village, and after Mr. Rothgen died, he lived on in the house with his mother. The home was never kept up and looked very shabby. The Professor would go to the dump and pick up light bulbs. He removed something (tungsten) from the filaments, which he sold. When radio came in, after the First World War, he helped Mel Immekus and Lee Sohns build battery radios. The floor was littered with papers (he was a saver), and the inside of the house was never finished—only the studs were there. Chickens were kept in the house in one room. Nearly everyone in the village had stories about the Professor.

Everyone in the village called William Staffeld "Uncle Bill." He was a kindly man, and after school he would drive his wagon around, picking up various kids and taking them home in the wagon.

Mr. Immekus said he remembers E. Ray Tompkins well. Tompkins murdered his wife in the first apartment building in Whitefish Bay, 1700 East Chateau Place, and hid her body out in the woods. Tompkins was owner/manager of this building. Mr. Immekus was working for Bill Staffeld in the alley behind the building, grading the alley. Tompkins came out of the building and asked Mr. Immekus if he would help move a trunk from the apartment to Tompkins' car in the road. Mr. Immekus said no, since his boss was right there, but two other men, working for a private company, said they would help and did. (One wonders what those men thought the next day when they read the newspaper and must have realized what had been in the trunk!) Tompkins was arrested shortly after her body was found and died in the Criminally Insane Hospital. [The preceding chapter provides much more on this story.]

Chapter 18

THE WHITEFISH BAY RESORTS

THE OLD WHITEFISH BAY RESORT, BY LEWIS W. HERZOG

It was a gala night in the early summer of 1889, June 25 to be exact, with more than three hundred distinguished guests at the official opening of the New Pabst Whitefish Resort. At a nod from manager Fred G. Isenring, toastmaster George W. Peck, soon to be elected mayor of Milwaukee and the next year governor of Wisconsin, rose, and the inevitable after-dinner speaking was underway. With ready wit, the author of "Pecks Bad Boy" discovered that "the north shore area of Milwaukee is indeed the original Garden of Eden." But even Paradise needs a benefactor whose liberality "has provided this beautiful garden," said the next speaker, A.W. Rich, "and has provided this beautiful resort—Captain Frederick Pabst."

Those who sat close to the good captain may have noted the ghost of a smile cross his face as he recalled the discussions he and his associates had had about the advisability of investing some $30,000 in this venture. The Pabst Brewing Company as such was only three months old—prior to March 1889 it had been the Best Brewing Co. The captain had long had a dream of a spacious resort on beautiful Whitefish Bay to carry the company's new name and to dispense its amber brew exclusively; the others held that the site was too far (five miles) from Milwaukee to attract large crowds. Originally, the only means of access was the toll road, which wound along the lake bluff. When Guido Pfister and associates agreed to build and operate the famed steam Dummy Line to Whitefish Bay, the captain and his brother-in-law, Emil Schandein, decided to go ahead with their plans before some competitor beat them.

Patrons enjoying the grounds of the Pabst Whitefish Bay Resort on a sunny, warm afternoon. *Whitefish Bay Historical Society.*

The Steam Dummy, officially the Milwaukee and Whitefish Bay Railway, went into service in 1888, but the work of erecting the pavilion and improving the grounds and beach was not completed until virtually one day of the official opening. As Captain Pabst mused, the speakers droned on. Colonel Jerome Watrous closed the program with his customary elegance, and the diners descended the broad stairs to the parlor and the pavilion proper, where many remained to dance to the music of an Italian orchestra until long past midnight. The public opening on Sunday, June 30, was advertised in Milwaukee newspapers over the signature of Fred Isenring, proprietor. Pabst, having no desire to operate the resort, had given him a five-year lease. The crowds began to arrive at an early hour on Sunday morning. Some came on the brand-new steamboat *Cyclone*, which made four trips from the Grand Avenue Bridge to the resort's dock at Whitefish Bay at the foot of Henry Clay Street. The easy grades of the crisscross paths led to the summit. Some came along the toll road, the Lake Avenue Turnpike, in their own or rented carriages or by horse-drawn bus. But the greatest number came on the Dummy Line, which ran trains every forty-five minutes during the day and evening right to the terminal across the road from the entrance to the park.

Regardless of means of transportation, they all arrived at the same rendezvous—a wooden structure built in the resort mode of the day. The ground floor was divided into four large apartments. Two were wings, seventy feet long, of a circular barroom of equal size from which broad stairs led to the second-floor dining room. Just north of the pavilion stood an octagonal bandstand where Professor Bach's military band rendered al fresco entertainment, and along the paths between the pavilion and the edge of the bluff were scattered the round white toadstool tables, many surrounded by groups of round white seats, surrounding the white stool tables, at which the visitor could sip his beer at leisure while looking out over the blue waters of Lake Michigan.

Eating, drinking and listening were the order of the day and the evening, too. Never in the twenty-six years of the resort's history (aside from at its opening) was there public dancing. That was left to Welcome Park and Jefferson Park—small pavilions within a stone's throw that got the over-flow trade and passed out of the picture within a few years. The New Resort was a success overnight. For some unknown reason, the owners tried to give it the "ritzy" name of Bellevue, but no one ever seemed to call it anything but the Whitefish Bay Resort. Isenring was a good host, and his five seasons of operation were generally successful. He had something of the promoter in him, trying such stunts as balloon ascensions to increase the crowds. After his wife died in 1893, he turned over the resort to his successor, the fabulous Henry Konopka.

Konopka was a Russian immigrant, reputed to be of noble birth, who had lost a fortune in South Dakota flax farms when they had been destroyed by prairie fires. He was sixty-five and a storekeeper at the Pabst Brewery when he took over as head of the resort. His decade of operation was the heyday of that establishment, the last ten years before the automobile began to change the entertainment habits of the nation. Konopka was a large man with white hair and beard, was a personality, suave, resourceful and deeply religious. It was said that he stood with head bowed while saying a silent grace before he sat down to a solitary meal in the crowded dining room. An epicure at heart, he personally supervised the kitchens and the wine cellar. A wine list from his regime shows the finest imported Champagne at $3.50 a quart and vintage wines for half that amount.

Following the World's Fair in Chicago in 1893, Ferris wheels became the rage all over the country. The Whitefish Bay Resort got one in 1895, a modest ten-car job erected at the extreme north end of the park. The

Pabst Whitefish Bay Resort. *Whitefish Bay Historical Society.*

Opposite, bottom: The Ferris wheel at the Whitefish Bay Resort, located at the north end of the property. *Whitefish Bay Historical Society.*

entrepreneurs of this device profited in two ways—from tickets sold to riders and from revenue from local firms who paid to place their names on the canvas tops of revolving cars.

The years seemed to speed by more rapidly as the end of the century approached. In 1898, the electric streetcars reached Whitefish Bay, and the Dummy Line now owned by the Electric Company passed out of existence. Summertime service featured open cars like the Marguerite with signs on the side of the roofs that spelled out names in electrically lighted letters a foot high. The streetcars could handle a big volume of traffic. It was not unusual of a Sunday to see the resort swarming with ten thousand people, and there were times, not infrequent, when the park's eighteen acres were strained to

hold almost half again that number. Sometimes when would-be visitors saw the tremendous crowds from the window, they just stayed aboard as the car made the loop at the terminal and went back home again.

Just after the turn of the century, Konopka introduced outdoor movies. A hand-cranked projector, set up on the steps leading to the circular bar, flashed the early "flickers" on a screen erected at the edge of the bluff. But this was not as successful as the drive-in theaters of fifty years later and was soon discontinued.

Konopka kept the property in excellent condition, more like a private estate than a public resort. An article in a Milwaukee newspaper in June 1902 said, "All work is now complete at the Whitefish Bay Resort. Flower beds are in summer attire, the oleander trees are in bloom and Mr. Konopka has added new effects in illumination of park and buildings. Joe Clauder's band and the famous quintet play daily from afternoon to evening."

An advertisement published just before the Fourth of July in the same year told of the mammoth fireworks display and announced that the steamer *Naomi* would leave the dock at the Pabst Building on Grand Avenue at 11:00 a.m., 2:00 p.m. and 7:00 p.m., with Clauder's band playing on the 2:00 p.m. trip. Many must have read this with regret for it meant that the steamer *Bloomer Girl* of tender memory was no longer making the Whitefish Bay run as it had for many seasons. Through the years, many craft had made the trip from the Grand Avenue docks, down the Milwaukee River, out past the breakwater and then "over the waves" to the bay. The round-trip fare was twenty-five cents, and bicycles were carried free. Some seasons, two boats ran the route. Among the other boats were: *Skater*, *R.J. Gordon*, *Barry*, *Eagle*, *Oval Agitator* and *Chequamegon*.

MISCELLANEOUS FACTS ABOUT THE WHITEFISH BAY RESORT

Fred G. Isenring bought Fernwood Cottage from Dr. T.W. Williams in 1889. Pabst Brewing Company bought Fernwood Cottage from Fred Isenring in 1891, changing its name to Edgewood Family Resort. The Edgewood was used to house the help needed to operate the Whitefish Bay Inn, including cooks, maids, bartenders and waiters. Edgewood was torn down in 1915.

Isenring bought the property for the Whitefish Bay Resort on April 1, 1877, for $1,600. He sold it to Pabst Brewing Company in November

1888 for $20,000. Fred then leased the property from Pabst and managed the resort.

While operating the resort, Fred Isenring lived with his family in a house near the north bandstand. His daughter Hattie was born there on December 11, 1880. When Henry Konopka took over management of the resort in 1894, this house was moved out of the park to the southwest corner of Lexington Boulevard and North Lake Drive. Konopka lived in the relocated residence, presumably until the resort was closed.

When Henry Konopka managed the resort, Eddie Klem reported to him. Klem was responsible for all bartenders and waiters. Eddie's father sold tickets to enter the Ferris wheel.

Konopka managed the resort for ten years, 1894 to 1904 inclusive. He was then pensioned by the Pabst Brewing Company. After an illness in a hospital, he died and was buried in Union Cemetery (3174 North Teutonia). All expenses were taken care of by Gustav Pabst, as had been previous[ly] arranged.

When the Pabst Whitefish Bay Resort closed in 1915, the Pabst Brewing Company made arrangements that the following families should have homes on the former property: Ralph Feerick, Walter Militzer, Mrs. Mary Froedert, A.D.E. Spooner, Otto A. Boheim, Arthur Hansen and Benjamin F. Saltzstein.

A picture of the Welcoming Park train station that greeted visitors to the Pabst Whitefish Bay Resort. *Whitefish Bay Historical Society.*

Harry LeVine, who worked as a waiter at the resort as a young lad (fourteen or fifteen years of age) eventually purchased a portion of the former resort property and built his home at 5320 North Lake Drive in 1930. According to his son, Edward, Harry LeVine immigrated to the United States with his parents when he was about ten. "He was a self-made man, working as a bookkeeper before becoming owner of Rosenberg's Department Store." As a child, Edward recalls swimming in the lake almost every day and having to avoid remnants of the old resort pier.

An image of the Whitefish Bay Resort appears in *Prohibition*, a three-part, five-and-a-half-hour documentary film series released on PBS in 2011 directed by Ken Burns and Lynn Novick. The effect of Prohibition, which officially started in 1920, on the resort is the subject of speculation. The lengthy campaign to prohibit the sale of alcohol may have contributed to a loss of revenues from the resort.

Chapter 19

MUZZY, TELL ME ABOUT YOUR DOLLHOUSE[73]

BY GLORIA ROCKWOOD HOUGHTON, 2006

This story was told by Gloria Houghton to her grandkids. Her grandkids knew her and her husband as "Muzzy and Dousi" rather than be confused with "Mommy and Daddy." Gloria published a compendium of her stories in 2006 in a book entitled Muzzy, Tell Me a Memory.

Do you remember how you learned about Santa Claus? I remember my experiences with Santa very vividly. It goes all the way back to 1928, when I was four years old in Milwaukee, Wisconsin.

My favorite game with my best friend, Nancye Jean, was to sit on the running board of my father's car, winter or summer, and play magic wishing ring. We each had glass rings from Woolworth's 5 & 10 cents store. We called them our wishing rings. We would rub them and make wishes, and usually the wishes would come true. I was practical, so my first wish was for an identical wishing ring, just in case I lost the one I was wearing. We would wish for balloons or tricycles or doll buggies, but nothing fancy like the toys on television today.

In December 1928, Nancye Jean and I were playing magic wishing ring as usual. Nancye Jean wished to know if Santa Claus were real. Her big brother John had told her that there wasn't a real Santa Claus. Of course he was real because our kindergarten teacher had told us he was coming to our school the next day. In Wisconsin, kindergarten is mandatory for two years; in fact, America's first kindergarten was in Watertown, Wisconsin. Nancye Jean and I attended four-year-old kindergarten every afternoon.

Gloria is pictured sitting in a goat cart in 1930. Milwaukee-area photographers canvased neighborhoods with their animal-drawn carts, offering to sell photographs of children in interesting poses. *Debby Houghton Schmidt.*

The next day, Schuster's Department Store sent a flatbed trailer to our school. Santa and one reindeer were on the trailer when our teacher led us outside to talk to Santa. Santa smelled like beer, and his reindeer was so old and his fur coat looked moth eaten. Santa tried to pull the reindeer down with a rope, but the reindeer just balked. How is that animal going to jump on our rooftop, click, click, click, if he can't even walk when Santa pulls him? Santa only had four fingers on his right hand. How could he possibly make all those toys without all his fingers? Nancye Jean and I were not impressed.

We told my mother about our disappointment, and she said, "Oh, that was just a helper. I'll take you to the Boston Store on Saturday to see the REAL Santa Claus." We were back sitting on the running board when I whispered to Nancye Jean my plan to discover if this Santa Claus was real.

It was a cold Saturday when we stood outside in the snow and waited for the Boston Store to open. The store window was filled with Lionel Electric Trains going in every direction. All the little boys liked the trains, but we couldn't wait to get inside to see the dolls and meet the real Santa Claus.

A store window with Lionel Toy Trains, perhaps similar to what Gloria and Nancye Jean observed on their visit to the Boston Store. Lionel began transitioning to a new line and look of trains in 1924. *Wikipedia Commons.*

We stood in a long line, and my mother gave two quarters to Santa's helper at the cash register. She put the money in a little black tube that raced up to the ceiling and out of sight. Then she yelled, "Two four-year girls." Two packages wrapped in brown paper came down a chute, and she handed them to us. "Here are your presents from Santa Claus." I stared at her and said, "If they are presents from Santa, why did my mother have to pay a quarter for them." She just told us to keep on walking, and we finally had our turn to see Santa Claus.

Now Nancye Jean and I could carry out our plan. When the wooden gate was open, we charged at Santa and jumped on his lap. We each whispered what we wanted in his ear. He nodded and asked if we had been good little girls. We told him we had been good. Then Nancye Jean said that she still wet the bed sometimes. Santa just laughed and said she was still good. We liked him because he smelled good and had all his fingers. He said he would certainly bring us our wish.

We rode the Wells Street Streetcar home, and my mother kept asking what we had wished Santa to bring us. We would never tell. This was our way to find out if Santa Claus were real. For two weeks, we kept our secret.

These were the days when children went to bed early on Christmas Eve and parents set up the Christmas tree and decorated it for a surprise. Just as my mother tucked me in bed, she asked, "Now what was it you told Santa Claus you wanted." I figured it was safe to tell her because Santa had already begun his journey. "Nancye Jean and I asked Santa to bring us each a dollhouse because our wishing rings never gave us a dollhouse. In kindergarten they have wonderful doll houses made of orange crates and we want our own dollhouses." Mother kissed me good night and closed the door.

I later learned that pandemonium broke loose. How do you find a dollhouse on Christmas Eve in 1928 when stores are closed? My mother and Mrs. Wilson stayed home and trimmed the trees. They sent our fathers out to try to find orange crates or dollhouses. It was hopeless, but the men finally found a drugstore open that sold paper dolls and they bought two paper doll books as a last resort.

On Christmas morning I gasped at the beautiful tree with real lights on it, and I quickly looked around for the dollhouse that didn't exist. There were other gifts under the beautiful tree, but no dollhouse. Mother gave me the paper doll book with a letter from Santa attached. She read it to me. "If you take very good care of this paper doll for a whole year, I will bring you a dollhouse next year. Love, Santa." I knew then that there was no real Santa Claus. "Well, Santa Claus must be left handed, Mother," I said. She asked me why I said that. Although I couldn't read, I knew that my mother slanted her letters backwards because she was left handed, so Santa must be left handed too because his letters looked like my mother's writing. Nancye Jean's brother John had been right.

A year passed, and it was Christmas 1929. The stock market had crashed, but it didn't affect my parents because they didn't have any stock anyway. They didn't have any money, either. I was now five years old and in advanced kindergarten. Nancye Jean and I still kept our wishing rings as our favorite game.

"I know what I'm getting for Christmas, Nancye Jean. I'm getting five smocked dresses. All fall my mother has been measuring me, and she keeps smocking every minute she has." If you are five years old, you DON'T want clothes for Christmas. You certainly don't want smocked dresses. She would wrap the dresses in tissue paper and hide them in her bottom dresser drawer. I was certain that she would tell me that Mrs. Santa Claus had smocked them.

On Christmas Eve, I went to bed early, and I could hear my parents busily trimming the tree. On Christmas morning, when I went into the living room expecting to see five smocked dresses under the Christmas tree, I was completely shocked. There was the most beautiful dollhouse in the whole world, and it wasn't made of orange crates. It was white with green shutters and a green roof. There was a red chimney and a red fireplace. There were real electric Christmas tree lights in the dollhouse.

I pulled up my little chair and began crying. I had never wished for anything so beautiful in my life. My wishing ring could never create this dollhouse. Santa Claus could never make anything this beautiful. Mother took me on her lap and told me that she had made five smocked dresses for a carpenter's little girl. In exchange, he had built this dollhouse for me. My mother's wonderful sewing had paid off, and she was my real Santa Claus.

The first thing I noticed was the dining room table that opened and had a leaf in it. Then there was the tiny silverware and the tiny china. I played with everything, and it was a week before I saw Nancye Jean's dollhouse. Her mother had found her dollhouse at Goodwill and fixed it up too. She had a grandfather clock and a roll of miniature toilet paper, but otherwise our houses were similar.

I played with my beloved dollhouse until I went away to college. Then my mother sold it, and it passed through three families before I saw it again. When our daughter Betsy was five years old, we began to track down the house and bought it back. It was in complete disrepair, but my mother and I repaired and repainted it. This was in 1954 in Wisconsin. Betsy was thrilled with the house

Gloria Rockwood in patriotic costume, taken in 1932. *Elizabeth Fulmer.*

just as I had been. We moved to Florida in 1955, and the dollhouse came along. Daughters grow up. After years of rough service, the dollhouse was relegated to the garage. Finally, when the doors broke off at the hinges, the remaining parts and pieces were stored away, high up in the rafters.

In 1983, our granddaughter Amy was five years old. She preferred playing with her puppy dog, Moxie, and the pet opossum she wore in her hair. The dollhouse still languished in the rafters playing host to spiders and roaches.

In 1999, when I was seventy-five years old, a miraculous thing happened. On Christmas morning, our daughter and son-in-law brought the seventy-year-old dollhouse and put it under the tree. They had been painting and scraping and mending seventy years of neglect for three months. They let me have the joy of furnishing it the way I wanted, and it has been a labor of love.

Everything in this dollhouse has a hidden meaning. All nine of our grandchildren are represented. Nothing was put in this house that does not have a story connected to it. There is even a roll of toilet paper in the right color and the right size. I photographed the pictures in our house, reduced

November 1904, Northern Wisconsin hunting party. The boy holding the rabbit he shot is Ellsworth Warren Rockwood ("Bud" Rockwood, 1898–1956). The woman aiming the gun is Adeline Elizabeth Hill Rockwood (1868–1940), and the man third from right is Daniel Ellsworth Rockwood (1861–1946). (The man at far right appears to be holding a "trip wire" to take the photograph.) *Elizabeth Fulmer.*

them in size and installed them. All of our hobbies are included and as many memories of sixty years of marriage as I could squeeze in the door.

I believe in Santa Claus now because I have seen his love in my mother's gift and in my daughter's restoration of my favorite childhood toy. Yes, and my husband is my real Santa Claus because he has paid the bills for whatever I wished for. My magic wishing ring is really my wedding ring today. It has answered all I could possibly wish for on this earth.

Mrs. Gloria Rockwood Houghton died on September 16, 2011. The family donated the dollhouse to the Harry P. Leu House Museum in Orlando, Florida.

Chapter 20

BABY IN THE MILWAUKEE RIVER

BY GLORIA ROCKWOOD HOUGHTON, 2006

I never had a broken bone, but I did have a serious accident on July 4, 1934. We moved to Whitefish Bay June 1, 1934, three months before my tenth birthday. My parents had just purchased Ott's Pharmacy, and they knew July 4 would be a very busy day for both of them. What could they do with me? Mother called Mrs. Wilson, my early childhood friend's mother, and asked what the Wilson family would be doing for the holiday. I had not seen Nancye Jean for two years, so I was excited about spending the day with the Wilsons. They were going to Blue Mound Country Club (a public golf club) for a holiday picnic. I joined their family, and it was fun to play with Nancye Jean again. Father George Oliver Wilson and fifteen-year-old son John were on the golf course after lunch.

Nancye picked up an extra golf club. I was standing behind her when she decided to swing the club. It connected with my left eye with a powerful crash. There was blood everywhere. I screamed, "Take me to a doctor. Take me to a hospital." The Wilson family were devout Christian Scientists, and Mrs. Wilson took me in her arms and said, "If God wants you to be blind, that is God's will."

I was a Baptist, and I wanted to see a DOCTOR, and the sooner the better. It seemed as if it took hours before Mr. Wilson was found on the golf course. He said he would not drive me to a doctor or to a hospital. Then I said, "Well, at least drive me home." Whitefish Bay was a long distance from Blue Mound Country Club, and this would ruin everyone's picnic. Nevertheless, they couldn't stop all the bleeding, so Mr. Wilson drove me to my father's drugstore.

My father took one look at all the blood. He knew Columbia Hospital was about six miles away. Because it was a holiday, he knew that all the doctors in the bay were on vacation. Then he remembered that a veterinarian on Silver Spring Drive had told him he would be open. In three minutes, I was on the table in the veterinarian's clinic. He cleaned me up and said he would need to take stitches from my nose to the outside of my left eyelid. I remembered my mother's anathema of stitches, and I asked if he could use butterfly bandages to prevent a scar. He said, "Absolutely no. There will be a scar from your nose across your eyelid." However, the scar would be in the crease of the eyelid, so it would fade eventually when I grew older. He said that the scar was incidental compared to blindness. There was so much blood that I could not see anything with my left eye. I wore a patch on my eye and the next day was examined by a regular specialist. For three weeks, I had a patch before they could determine what had happened to my eyesight.

When they finally removed all the stitches and bandages, everything was a blur. However, I guess God didn't intend for me to be blind because my vision returned to 20/20 by the time I entered fifth grade in the fall. It was the last time I ever saw Nancye Jean and the Wilson family.

There was an adventure that happened shortly after the golf club fiasco. On my tenth birthday, I received two special gifts, my Shirley Temple doll and my blue and silver twenty-eight-inch World bicycle. I had the bandages off my eye, but I still wasn't ready to ride my bicycle. On the last Sunday in August, my mother suggested that I invite my friend Phyllis Weisel to come out to spend the afternoon with me. She had been my best friend when we lived on Prospect Avenue.

Phyllis' mother put her on the #15 streetcar on Oakland Avenue. The streetcar tracks ended on Silver Spring Drive a block east of our drugstore. I met Phyllis at the streetcar and took her to our apartment. Phyllis did not like dolls, so Shirley Temple was not interesting to her. I couldn't ride my new bike until my vision was completely back. They didn't wear bike helmets in those days, so it would be dangerous if I fell.

Then I suggested that she might like to take a hike to the Milwaukee River, four blocks west of the drugstore. We walked along Silver Spring and crossed the Port Washington Road. It is a busy highway today, but in 1934 two little ten-year-old girls could safely walk across the highway. We slid down the bank to the Milwaukee River. We looked around for sticks and finally found two nice sticks so that we could pretend to be fishing. We splashed the water on each other and had the usual fun of poking the sticks into the river. Suddenly, my stick hit something, and I pulled it to shore. It was a full-size

The Port Silver Diner was located at 5260 North Port Washington Road. It is now the site of Burger King. *Whitefish Bay Historical Society.*

dead baby. At first I thought it was a rubber doll. Then I looked closely and saw that it had its umbilical cord still attached to its stomach. I could not tell if it [was] a boy or girl because it was lying on its side. Phyllis and I looked at it very closely as we pulled it on shore with our sticks. Then we ran screaming up the hill. "We've found a dead baby. We've found a dead baby!" We ran the four blocks to my father's drugstore, and he came running back to the river with us.

By this time, a crowd had gathered on the corner of Silver Spring and the Port Washington Road. Someone had gone into the Port Silver Diner and called the police. They were already there when we arrived. The police wanted to talk to me, but my father said, "Absolutely no." So they talked to him instead. My father found someone in the crowd he knew who would drive Phyllis home. One police car drove us back to the drugstore, and the other car took care of details at the scene. My father winked at the policeman and said, "She has found a rubber doll in the river." I kept saying, "But, Daddy, it was a dead baby, not a doll."

My father probably never took any courses in psychology at Marquette, but I think he did the right thing. He said, "Repeat after me—I found a doll in the river." Whenever I would ask about the dead baby, he would again say, "I found a doll in the river." Later, my cousins would ask me to tell them the story about finding the dead baby, and I would repeat, "I found a doll in the river." I am sure the story was in the newspapers because kids would ask me in school, "What about the dead baby you found?" I would answer, "I found a doll in the river."

This 1938 picture shows Gloria standing in front of her parents' vehicle. Her dad's pharmacy at the corner of East Silver Spring Drive and Diversey Boulevard is in the background. *Deborah Houghton Schmidt.*

How did I know about umbilical cords? My mother told me when I was nine years old. We went to visit Pauline Lazar's new baby, and Mother showed me the tape on the baby's tummy and explained the word umbilical. When did I ever see Phyllis Weisel again? We never talked on the phone, and we never discussed the baby we had found. Perhaps her mother used my father's method of brainwashing. Whenever I think about that afternoon, I still repeat, "I found a doll in the river." No nightmares and no traumatic flashbacks ever occurred. It must have been an amazing summer for my parents to survive the golf club and the river accident.

Editor's note: I searched several times for a newspaper account of this incident but was unable to find anything. I suppose that's to be expected. It is likely that the baby was aborted or born alive and thrown in the river. Such incidents do not appear to have been widely reported back then.

Chapter 21

EARLY SETTLERS AND FARMERS OF WFB

THE CONSAUL, FUNKE, GRAMS, KAESTNER, LEU, MOHR, PATZA AND STEFFEN FAMILIES

There are many early farmhouses nestled in the neighborhoods of Whitefish Bay. These surviving homes often stand out and represent good examples of farmhouses from the 1800s. The historic preservation commission has been researching the families that originally occupied these homes. These families were among the earliest settlers in the village. Their families often became intertwined through marriage, perhaps because of their relative isolation but also because they shared common nationalities and cultures.

This chapter is divided into the "Northsiders," those families living north of Silver Spring Drive, and the "Southsiders," those families generally living south of Henry Clay Street. While the chapter doesn't cover all of the early Whitefish Bay farms, hopefully it provides a good overview.

FRED AND FERDINAND GRAMS

The Gramses were among the earliest residents of the area. Christopher and Rosina (Boock or Borck) Grams farmed twenty acres on what is now the southwest corner of Dean Road and Lake Drive in present Fox Point. They were born in Prussia, according to the census. It is believed that they were from the Mecklenburg area of Germany, similar to a

Opposite: The Northsiders. *Whitefish Bay Historical Society.*

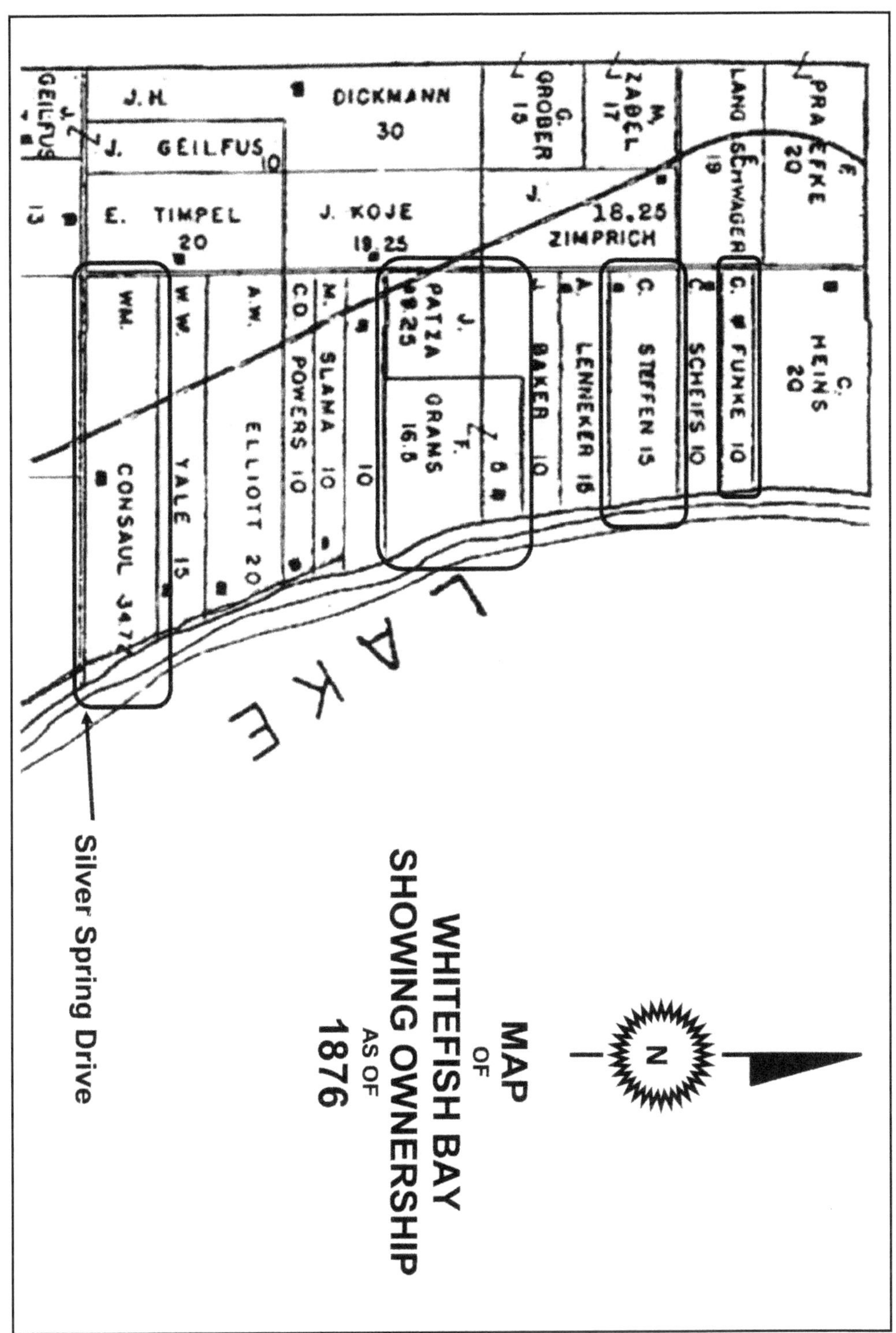
MAP
OF
WHITEFISH BAY
SHOWING OWNERSHIP
AS OF
1876
N
Silver Spring Drive
LAKE
J. GEILFUS 13
J.H. DICKMANN 30
J. GEILFUS 10
E. TIMPEL 20
J. KOJE 19.25
G. GROBER 15
M. ZABEL 17
J. ZIMPRICH 18.25
E. LANDSCHWAGER 19
F. PRAEFKE 20
WM. CONSAUL
W.W. YALE 15
A.W. ELLIOTT 20
C.O. POWERS 10
M. SLAMA 10
10
J. PATZA 19.25
F. GRANS 16.5
BAKER 10
A. LENNEKER 15
C. STEFFEN 15
C. SCHEIFS 10
G. FUNKE 10
C. HEINS 20

Anna (Engel) Grams. *Whitefish Bay Historical Society.*

Frederich Grams. *Whitefish Bay Historical Society.*

number of other farmers in the area.[74] They had at least three children, Frederich (Frederick), Christopher and Minnie.

In 1864, Frederick acquired sixteen and a half acres in Whitefish Bay and moved onto the farm. Frederick immigrated to the United States with his parents. He married Anna Engel in 1869. Anna was also from Mecklenburg. Their farm extended between what is now Lake Drive and Lake Michigan, part of which has become Klode Park. It is believed that their farmhouse was built in anticipation of their marriage—or shortly thereafter. Frederick and Anna had at least nine children (including Louise, Lillie, Alvina, Ferdinand, Elsie, Annie, Hulda and Hattie).

Frederick died on July 2, 1912, at age seventy. He left his widow, Anna, and nine children and an estate worth approximately $18,700. Anna spoke only German at the estate settlement and said that only their youngest child, who was then age nineteen, was still living at home with her. She further testified that she had two additional children (Louis and Fred) who died as babies. Each descendant received $1,764 as his/her share of inheritance.

The farmland was eventually sold—it is likely that it was sold to settle the estate. The original house was moved from the farm site to 5967 North Berkeley Boulevard in 1925 and placed on a new foundation.

Gottfried and Caroline Funke

At the time of the 1870 census, Gottfried was forty-six—a stone mason from Prussia. His wife, Caroline, was thirty-five—also from Prussia. They had two children, Charles and Lena. Their name was listed as "Funk" but in later censuses and other documents was listed as "Funke."

In 1866, they purchased approximately ten acres between Santa Monica Boulevard (then Richards Street) and the lake.

Charles married Mary Kassebaum in 1881. He was reportedly a plumbing contractor. Lena married Heinrich Post, who died in 1919. She remarried, but her new husband's name is unknown.

Gottfried died in 1890 and Caroline in 1923. They are buried in the Town of Milwaukee Cemetery with their daughter Lena and her first husband.

The house at 5932 North Santa Monica Boulevard is their original farmhouse.

Joseph and Magdalena Patza

At the time of the 1870 census, Joseph was fifty-one—originally a stonemason from Bohemia. His wife, Magdalena, was thirty-four—also from Bohemia. They had two children at the time, Mary Anna (six) and Joseph (three). Magdalena was the daughter of John and Theresa Sweda.

They purchased approximately ten acres on the southwest corner of Santa Monica Boulevard and Montclair Avenue.

By the 1880 census, they had two additional children, Benjamin and Anna (Annie). Anna (Annie) married Henry Lemke, and they later lived in the house. Their daughter Genevieve passed along some of the information about her family to Mimi Bird.

Joseph died in the year 1900 and Magdalena in 1914. They and other family members are buried in Calvary Cemetery—the surname on the monument in the family plot is spelled "Paca," but "Patza" is the name on the individual gravestones.

CARL (CHARLES) AND FREDERICKA STEFFEN

The early Whitefish Bay farmhouse at 611 North Santa Monica Boulevard was built for Carl (Charles) Steffen and his family in the late 1860s or early 1870s. He appears in the 1870 census, shown as a farmer from Prussia who was forty years of age, married to Hanna, aged forty-two, with two children—August, aged twelve, and Franz, aged seven.

In the 1880 census, he again appears, but his wife's name is shown as Fredericka, with one child, Henry, aged sixteen. While the names are somewhat confusing, Fredericka appears to be the same person as Hanna, and Henry is likely Franz. August would likely have moved out of the residence by that time. The 1892 census for Whitefish Bay shows another child of Carl Steffen and his wife—daughter Louise (Lizzie) Alwine. Lizzie married Otto August Georg Voeks, son of Johanna (Krueger) and August Voeks, on October 25, 1892. They lived at 524 East Day Avenue.

Carl and his family eventually relocated to what is now 531 East Day Avenue. He died there in 1897, but his wife continued to live there until her death in 1903.

Carl and Friedericka are buried in the Town of Milwaukee Cemetery, along with a substantial number of descendants and other Steffens.

THE CONSAULS

The Consaul family came from New York in the 1800s, apparently from the Schenectady area. Descendants state the Consauls lived for a time in Toledo, Ohio, prior to settling here. William Consaul, born in 1796, married Eliza Henry in 1816, and they had eleven children—seven of whom lived beyond their infancy.

In 1853, they acquired thirty acres of farmland in an area of present Whitefish Bay currently bordered by Lake Michigan on the east, Santa Monica Boulevard on the west, Silver Spring Drive on the south and Lake View Avenue on the north. At one time, they also owned fifteen acres to the north of Lake View Avenue but sold that property to Gallus Isenring.

The oldest of the surviving Consaul residences is at 716 East Silver Spring Drive. It is believed that this was the original William Consaul residence. The home may have been built in 1856, according to the current owner's research. However, there is a possibility that the home may have been built

William Consaul's residence at 716 East Silver Spring—oldest surviving residence in Whitefish Bay. *Whitefish Bay Historic Preservation Commission.*

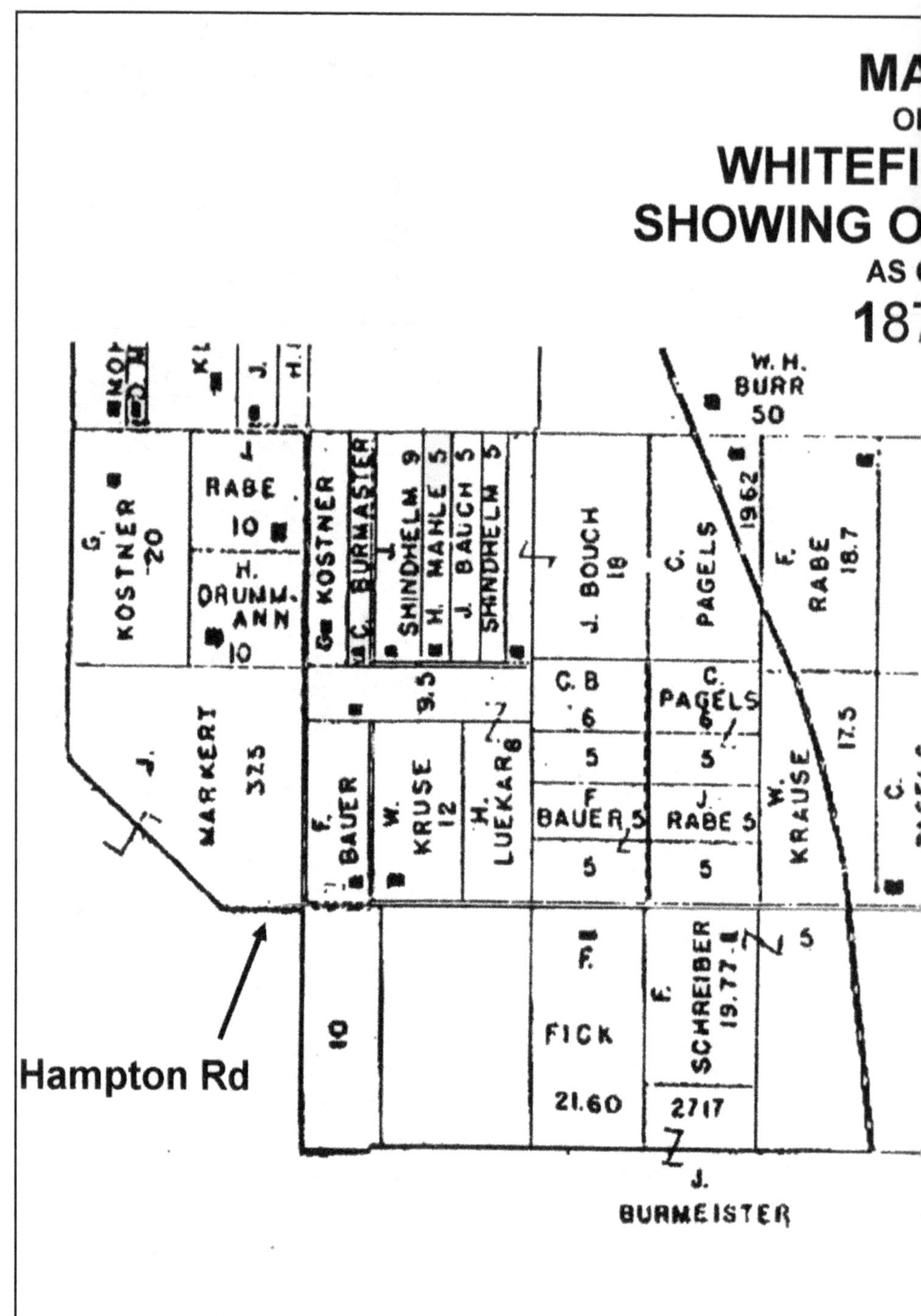
MA
O
WHITEFI
SHOWING O
AS
18
W. H. BURR 50
G. KOSTNER 20
RABE 10
H. DRUMM-ANN 10
G. KOSTNER
C. BURMASTER
J. SHINDHELM 9
H. MAHLE 5
J. BAUCH 5
SHINDHELM 5
J. BOUCH 18
C. PAGELS
1962
F. RABE 18.7
J. MARKERT 325
9.5
F. BAUER
W. KRUSE 12
H. LUEKAR 8
C. B 6
5
BAUER 5
C. PAGELS 6
J. RABE 5
W. KRAUSE
17.5
10
F. FICK
21.60
F. SCHREIBER 19.77
2717
J. BURMEISTER
Hampton Rd

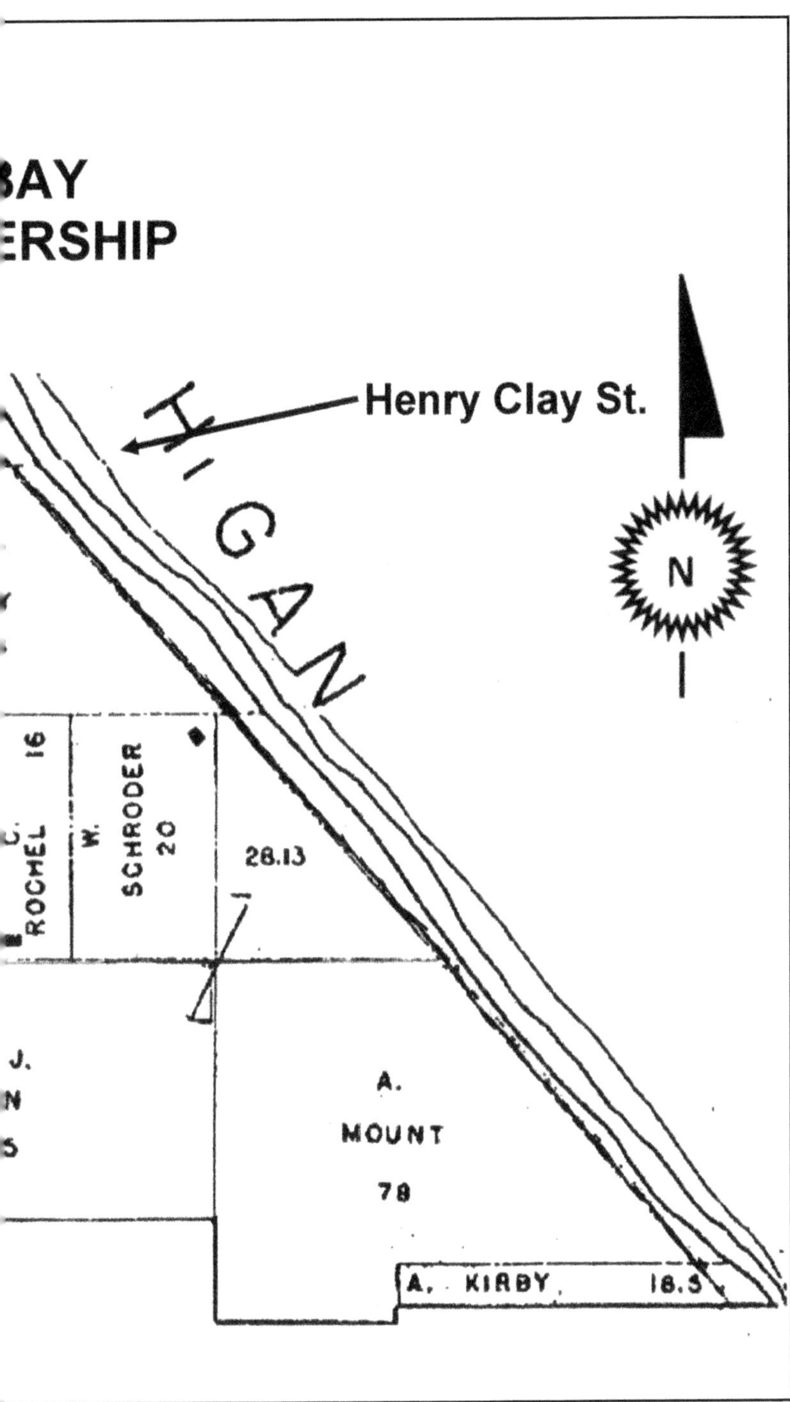

The Southsiders. The map was hand drawn by Arthur Rabe and displays property ownership in the southern portion of the village in 1876. *Whitefish Bay Historical Society.*

somewhat earlier. Real estate records indicate that William Consaul Sr. left a house to his son William H. upon his death in 1855. If this is the house cited in the real estate transfer, it existed prior to 1855. In any case, it appears likely that this is the oldest surviving residence in Whitefish Bay.

After his father's death, William H. Consaul owned and occupied this home with his wife, Ruth. Their children, Mary Jane and Frank W. Consaul, were both born in this house. Mary Jane was born in February 1859 and Frank W. in 1862.

The house was later conveyed to Mary Jane Consaul and her husband, Lewis F. Scheife (also referred to in some documents as Schief). In 1894, the house became the Kilbourn Fresh Air Society Home for young city children brought out to the country to spend the spring and fall months. At the time, most of the land surrounding this house was open farm field.

Eliza died in April 1837, and William remarried Hannah M. Everts. It does not appear that he had any children by his second wife.

The 1850 census shows William Consaul, aged fifty-five and employed as a contractor, living in the Fifth Ward of the city of Milwaukee. At the time of the census, he was married to his second wife, Hanna M. (née Everts), age forty-eight. It appears that most of William Sr.'s children moved with them to the Milwaukee area. William died on March 17, 1855, and is buried in the Town of Milwaukee Cemetery.

The 1860 Town of Milwaukee census shows Hannah M. Consaul (recently widowed) and her stepdaughter, Susan M. Consaul (twenty-one), who married Daniel W. Chipman in 1861. Also shown were William H. Consaul (forty), listed as a farmer, and his wife, Rose (also referred to as Ruth, thirty-six, originally from England) and their four children.

In 1864, William H. Consaul and his brother, Captain Theodore, began commercial pound net fishing in Whitefish Bay.[75] Their business was later sold to William's son-in-law, Lewis Scheife, who then supplied the Whitefish Bay Resort and other establishments with whitefish. It is likely that the village's name originated because of their fishing enterprise.

William H. and his wife Ruth had additional children in the years following the 1860 census. The family Bible, formerly in the possession of Mrs. Olive (Scheife) Packard Lowry and later held by her daughter, Mary Jane Scherzueger of Portland, Oregon, lists their children, who included Mary Jane, who was born February 7, 1859, and married Lewis F. Scheife in 1884, son of Karl and Caroline Scheife, also of Whitefish Bay. Mary Jane died on December 23. Both she and her husband are buried in the Town of Milwaukee Cemetery (located just north of the current Bayshore Town Center).

William H. Consaul died in 1889 and his wife in 1896. Both are also buried in the Town of Milwaukee Cemetery.

The Mohr Family

John Mohr is shown in the 1850 census as a farmer, age forty-eight, originally from Germany and living with his wife, Ava, and children, Philip and Andreas. Records indicate that John Mohr died in 1852. At the time of his death, he had twenty acres of land.

In 1861, John and Ava's son Philip Mohr married Dorthea (Doris) Rose, daughter of Johann and Anna Marie Rose, who farmed land located just north of the Mohr family. Philip was twenty-one at the time. The 1880 census shows them with nine children. Their first son, John, married Alvina Leu, daughter of Ludwig and Rosa Leu. They moved into Alvina's parents' home, still standing at 400 East Hampton Road. Their daughter, Adelaide, continued to live in the residence as late as 1992.

Philip and Dorthea Mohr's son William eventually became Whitefish Bay's first lamplighter. At least seventeen Mohrs are recorded as buried in the Town of Milwaukee Cemetery.

On September 25, 1925, the *Shorewood Radio* (forerunner of the *Whitefish Bay Herald*) reported that "Philip H. Mohr, 88 years old, has lived on his farm on Washington Avenue (now Henry Clay Street) for 61 years. The farm is about three blocks east of the Port Washington Road. His father came to this country 61 years ago from Germany, bought this farm land and lived there until his death, when it went to his son and grandson, in turn." The interview goes on to report how the Mohrs hunted bears and wolves on their property, hauled loads of cordwood to the City and sold them at the marketplace—now the site of Milwaukee's City Hall.

Philip Mohr's obituary (March 8, 1929) reported that he used to help his father bring farm produce and wood to the market in Milwaukee via oxen-drawn cart. It was necessary to ford the Milwaukee River at a spot in what is now Lincoln Park. During the Civil War, he served in the Wisconsin infantry.

The Kaestner home is presently located at 106 West Henry Clay Street. *Whitefish Bay Historic Preservation Commission.*

THE KAESTNER FAMILY

George Kaestner immigrated to Wisconsin from Germany. In 1849, he married Mary Mohr, daughter of John and Ava Mohr. They farmed land south of Henry Clay. Their son Henry and his wife, Alvina, built the house at 106 West Henry Clay Street. It originally stood on the south side of the street. Henry and Alvina's daughter, Clara, married Fred Mohr, a great-grandchild of John and Ava Mohr, and moved the house across the road to its present location.

THE LEU FAMILY

Julius Leu came to Milwaukee with his parents in 1865, married Pauline and farmed near Lancaster Street and Santa Monica for twenty years.

Picture of Julius and Pauline Leu. *Whitefish Bay Historical Society.*

Julius and Pauline's son, Ludwig, built a house at 400 East Hampton Road in 1886. It was moved to the north side of Hampton in 1889 and was later occupied by Adelaide Mohr, a granddaughter of Ludwig's, and her nephew and his wife, the Gordon Mohrs. Adelaide lived in the home until 1992. Ludwig also built the house at 519 East Hampton Road in about 1890.

VEGETABLE FARMERS

On census reports, all the Mohrs, Kaestner and Leu families were vegetable farmers. It is believed that their produce was sold at various farmers' markets in the city of Milwaukee. The accompanying photograph shows workers

Harvesting from Fred Mohr's vegetable farm. The workers are not identified but are thought to be members of the Mohr family. *Whitefish Bay Historical Society.*

(unidentified, but presumably members of the Mohr family) in the field on Fred Mohr's farmland.

In addition to building classic, sturdy homes, all lovingly maintained by their current owners, the three families contributed to the village's civic history. Julius Leu was a village trustee twice, from 1896 to 1899 and from 1908 to 1917. He also served as the village's street commissioner and headed its Department of Public Works. John and Ava Mohr's son Andrew became the treasurer of the Town of Milwaukee, and his son, William, was the village's first lamplighter.

Chapter 22

MOVERS AND SHAKERS FROM WHITEFISH BAY

BY THOMAS FEHRING

This chapter attempts to identify some of the people who lived in the village of Whitefish Bay and went on to achieve national and, in some cases, international prominence. As in any attempt like this, I'm certain that I missed many former residents who should have been included. I apologize for these omissions.

A. CRESSY MORRISON

I stumbled across Mr. Morrison quite by accident. I was writing an article for the "Preserving Our Past" column on WhitefishBayNOW. The article featured a modest house on East Day Avenue. Previous research on the former cottage indicated that it was originally owned by an A. Cressy Morrison. I didn't know anything about Morrison and decided to find out who he was.

Google and other Internet search engines are terrific tools, as we all know. They can provide us with amazing clues. However, they can also be frustrating—providing the user with more misses than hits. Fortunately, our Morrison was given a very distinctive middle name. When I typed his name into the search line, Google zeroed in on our man: Abraham Cressy Morrison. And I'm still amazed with the results. Morrison might be the most influential yet largely unknown person who has ever lived in Whitefish Bay. His interests and accomplishments are so broad that at first I believed I was finding links for both father and son. But as it turns out, they all refer to one remarkable man.

I'll start with the basic facts, most of which were taken from the *History of Milwaukee County*.[76] Abraham Cressy Morrison was born in Wrentham, Massachusetts, on December 6, 1864. He traveled extensively with his parents (California, Isthmus of Panama) before they were "met with reverses," and he had to "give up all educational advantages and devote himself to the serious problem of life" at age thirteen.

> *He drifted from retail dry goods to machinery and tools, from wholesale dry goods to work in a hotel, from a lawyer's office to syrups and molasses, from coals and wood to hard rubber and from there to a proprietary article called Maltine.*
>
> *The proprietary business*[77] *with the Maltine Manufacturing Company was not satisfactory in some respects, but during the short*

> *time he remained in their employ he was called upon to interview, on the subject of their wares, some seven thousand physicians and five thousand druggists.*

This provided him with a foundation into the technique of advertising and landed him a job with the Pabst Brewing Company, where he eventually became in charge of advertising/publicity, at the age of twenty-three.[78]

I also discovered that Morrison was an avid "wheelman" (bicyclist we'd call him today). He was an official in the League of American Wheelmen, serving as president of the Milwaukee Wheelmen and eventually being named vice-president in the national organization. He participated in long-distance races and finished "within the money" in several one-hundred-mile contests.

The Milwaukee to Whitefish Bay "run" was described by bicycling enthusiasts of the day as perhaps the most popular short run in the state. An early magazine for bicycle enthusiasts stated, "The road is always in prime condition and during the summer months good entertainment may be found at the Bay. The famous road begins in the extreme northeastern part of the city and follows a winding course of 5 miles along the lake shore."[79]

Morrison led local and national campaigns to improve roads (you can't cycle very well on dirt and gravel) and was appointed by the governor of Wisconsin to the Committee on Good Roads.

This image of the southern portion of the Pabst Whitefish Bay Resort shows a number of "Wheelmen" and their cycles to the left. Perhaps A. Cressy Morrison is among them. *Whitefish Bay Historical Society.*

A. Cressy Morrison at age thirty. *Photograph from* History of Milwaukee County, *1895.*

Morrison also had other interests. He wrote a history of Milwaukee for a publication by the local real estate companies and a chapter on the brewing industry that was itself included in the *History of Milwaukee County*. He also wrote some literary works—the *Story of Damon and Pythias* and *The Man Who Resembled Christ*. The first publication was adopted as the "authentic version of the Knights of Pythias and ran through several editions—nearly 200,000 copies."

An article in the *Milwaukee Journal* on August 29, 1896, provides us with some interesting Whitefish Bay connections. It describes a "coaching" party of the Milwaukee Wheelmen. The group left the Milwaukee Suburban Club and then biked to the Bellevue.

The Bellevue noted in the third sentence of the accompanying article is the name of the main building at the Pabst Whitefish Bay Resort. Note in particular the last sentence, which names, in addition to A. Cressy Morrison, Mr. and Mrs. Alonzo Fowle and Charles A. McGee.

We know that Alonzo Fowle and the father of Charles McGee were in the printing business together, and Alonzo Fowle's family lived at 624 East Day Avenue—across the street from Morrison's cottage at 615 East Day. We also know that a structure at 415 East Day Avenue was built in 1896 for the Whitefish Bay Club[80] and was used as a clubhouse for the Wheelmen.

And the connections get stronger. The printing business owned by Whitefish Bay's Alonzo Fowle, James McGee and Henry King produced an early coffee table–style book in 1892 entitled *Milwaukee: 100 Photogravures*. The first article in that book, written on Milwaukee's history, was by none other than A. Cressy Morrison!

It is evident that Morrison had exhibited significant writing skills in his work for Pabst in advertising and publicity. The chapter he wrote on Milwaukee's history for *Milwaukee: 100 Photogravures* might have been one of his

Coaching Party of Milwaukee Wheelmen.

The coaching party of the Milwaukee Wheelmen last evening was highly enjoyable. From the clubrooms the party proceeded to the Suburban club, where light refreshments were served. The party then proceeded to the Bellevue, where dancing was indulged in. ... Among the Whitefish Bay residents in attendance were Mr. and Mrs. R. A. McAllister, Mr. And Mrs. Alonzo Fowle, Chas. A. A. McGee, Henry F. Conchrens, Mr. and Mrs. James J. Perkins, Loiver Drebert, Mr. and Mrs. C. R. Gether and Mr. and Mrs. F. E. Baltes.

Morrison's Candidacy Popular

The strong boom of A. Cressy Morrison for president of the L. A. W. is receiving additional impetus in various parts of the country. The second vice-president of the big organization is being endorsed in a manner which indicates that he will go down to the winter meeting with the strongest support ever given to a western candidate. The latest evidence is offered by Editor J. M. Erwin of Bicycle News, one of the most influential writers on wheel topics. He says:

"There is talk of running our near neighbor, A. Cressy Morrison of Milwaukee, for president of the League of American Wheelmen at the next election. Even though Mr. Morrison lives in Milwaukee and not in Chicago we are for him. We do not have an opportunity to see Mr. Morrison very often, for he is very busy with evolving those weird and winding specimens of artistic advertising that tell us of the virtue of the Pabst product (which we already know) but we do realize that in Wisconsin he is the good kind king that looks benignly and wisely over the doings of the Badgers that are disposed to fight about half the time. And as for presence and dignity – well, in the language of the great Tooter Johnson, 'He is that.' Are we for Morrison? Well, just draw us for campaign expenses if the Pabst funds should ever run low."

Milwaukee Journal article from August 29, 1896.

This house at 415 East Day Avenue was originally used as a clubhouse for the Wheelmen. *Whitefish Bay Historic Preservation Commission.*

MILWAUKEE'S HISTORY

A. CRESSY MORRISON

For two hundred historical years, and for an untold period before, of which history gives no response to the inquirer, the present location of Milwaukee had been used as a peaceful meeting-place of the Indians of the entire surrounding country – the name Milwaukee meaning "universal council-grounds." The instinctive recognition of this location by the Indians as a most desirable and central meeting point, is the highest compliment which can be paid the geographical position of Milwaukee. It is now 193 years since Father De St. Cosme mentioned the name Milwaukee in his letter to the Bishop of Quebec, reporting a two day's rest at the mouth of the "Melwarik" River, which, undoubtedly, was his best rendition of the Indian name, which should be pronounced *Mahn-ak-wauk.*

If additional proof was needed that the aboriginal races had the highest appreciation of natural beauty and an inherent sense of the artistic in nature, this location of Milwaukee for the universal council-grounds would be irrefutable evidence. Milwaukee rests upon the entre circuit of the most beautiful bay and harbor on the great lakes, and the high bluffs, covered with their summer dress of green, rise in graceful undulations, like a velvet carpet, upon which the city rests. The streets run east and west, north and south, and are lined with beautiful shade trees, and the houses are surrounded by lawns of large dimensions. Like one great family, Milwaukeeans live happily without fences. This absence of fences makes the residence portion of the city like a vast park and impresses one with the neighborly social atmosphere which pervades both private and business intercourse.

The first permanent white settlers were Jacques Vieau and Solomon Juneau, Indian traders, who came in September, 1818. The name of Solomon Juneau is reverently held in the memory of every old settler in Milwaukee. His generous heart and open hand made him beloved by all, and at his death in Shawano, Wis., November 14, 1856, the Indians, who loved him as a father, grief stricken, "with stately tread and blackened faces, passed in review the corpse of their dead friend, and the chiefs in solemn council summoned their braces to attend his funeral." "Never," said old Augustin Grignon, "have I heard of this before." He was buried in Shawano by the Indians, but was afterwards removed to Milwaukee. His demise was sincerely mourned by the entire city.

The printing business owned by Whitefish Bay's Alonzo Fowle, James McGee and Henry King produced an early coffee table–style book in 1892 entitled *Milwaukee: 100 Photogravures*. The first article in that book, written on Milwaukee's history, was by none other than A. Cressy Morrison. *Whitefish Bay Historical Society.*

earliest non-work-related articles—and may have played an important role in shaping his later career.

The details of Abraham Cressy Morrison's later life are somewhat sketchy. However, it appears that he was able to take his experience with chemistry, pharmaceuticals, advertising and writing and morph them into some interesting endeavors. I have not been able to locate a full bio, but a short article written at the time of his death in 1951 fills some gaps:

> *A. CRESSY MORRISON, 86, retired former executive of the Union Carbide and Carbon Corp., died in Brooklyn Jan. 9*[, 1951]. *He was born at Wrentham, Mass., and had to leave school at 13 to earn money. While in his twenties he was in charge of publicity for the Pabst Brewing Co., and in 1897 became chairman of the committee on credits and collections of the National Wholesale Druggists Association and the committee on advertising of the Proprietary Association.*
>
> *Beginning in 1924 he offered prizes through the New York Academy of Sciences, of which he was president in 1938, totaling about $1,000 a year. The prizes were given for theses on solar and stellar energy. He was the author of* Man in a Chemical World, Encyclopedia of Superstition *and other books. He belonged to The Chemists' Club of New York.*

Other 'hits' on the web reveal that Morrison:

- Wrote *Damon and Pythias*, which was published in 1890 by King, Fowle & Co. of Milwaukee/Whitefish Bay and was given as a souvenir for the Knights of Pythias, provided compliments of Pabst Brewing Company. A reported twenty million copies were printed, to be "left on the doorstep of every house in all the cities of the United States with a population over 2,500."[81]
- Wrote *Man Does Not Stand Alone*, a condensed version of which ran in the *Reader's Digest*.
- Wrote "Seven Reasons a Scientist Believes in God"; *The Baking Powder Controversy*, Volumes 1 and 2; and "The League of Nations, Cartels and the Tariff."
- Was president of the New York Academy of Sciences in the late 1930s.

Some articles refer to Morrison as Dr. A. Cressy Morrison or as "Professor." He was a named a "Fellow" in the New York Academy of Sciences—a position generally held by esteemed scientists. However, his education was limited to "a public school education and a year in business college."[82]

A. Cressy Morrison later in life.

Cressy, as his intimate friends knew him, married the former Marguerite Snow of New York. They had a family summer residence on Deer Isle, located just southwest of Bar Harbor, Maine, where Morrison spent time entertaining and fishing.

In researching Abraham Cressy Morrison, I also came across an interesting tidbit about his sister, Cora Linn (Morrison) Daniels, who appears to have been a fascinating author. Born in 1852, she published, among other titles, a three-volume work entitled *The Encyclopaedia of Superstitions, Folklore, and the Occult Sciences of the World*, which is reported to be a comprehensive library of human belief and practice in the mysteries of life. An earlier work entitled *As It Is to Be* was published in 1892 by our good Whitefish Bay friends King, Fowle & Company of Milwaukee. And in 1899, she published a mystery entitled *The Bronze Buddha*, which included this dedication:

> *To My Beloved Brother,*
> *Abraham Cressy Morrison*
>
> *His name adorns my work*
> *as his character adorns his name*

This tale has connections, upon connections, upon connections!

I noted earlier that I believe Morrison may have been the most influential person to have lived in Whitefish Bay—with apologies to former governor Julius P. Heil and others. There are two reasons why I believe this may be true.

First, the A. Cressy Morrison Award, which he established in 1926 and was awarded annually until the mid-1990s by the New York Academy of Sciences, has had far-reaching consequences. For example, Hans Bethe,[83]

Recent photograph of A. Cressy Morrison's Cottage at 615 East Day Avenue. Who would have thought that this unimposing former cottage held such secrets? *Whitefish Bay Historic Preservation Commission.*

one of the recipients for his theory of the carbon cycle in stars, famously told the tale of competing for the Morrison Award "to liberate my mother's furniture from [Nazi] Germany." He received the Nobel Prize for the carbon cycle in 1967. It appears that at least three recipients of the Morrison award went on to be granted Nobel Prizes.

Second, Morrison's attempt to explain the existence of God from a scientific view triggered a debate that continues to this day. His essay on "Seven Reasons a Scientist Believes in God" and other works that he published, are widely quoted by both believers and nonbelievers in the search for answers.

HENRY HERMAN MCKINNIES JR. (AKA JEFFREY HUNTER)

Written by Jeff Aikin

Every spring, as Christians the world over celebrate the crucifixion and resurrection of the "King of Kings," Jesus Christ, Whitefish Bay residents can take pride in knowing that one of their own played the title role in the celebrated 1961 movie of the same name.

Henry Herman McKinnies Jr., Whitefish Bay High School class of 1945, played Jesus in the three-hour epic in what was perhaps his best-known, if not his most-acclaimed, movie role. Most will recall McKinnies by his Hollywood name, Jeffrey Hunter.

Hunter was born on November 25, 1926, in New Orleans. He was four years old when his family moved to Whitefish Bay. They initially lived at 5529 North Lydell Avenue and later moved to 4957 North Larkin Street.

Hunter's childhood home on Larkin was recently placed on Whitefish Bay's Architecture and Historic Inventory by the Historic Preservation Commission. The brick residence was built in 1941 by builder Roy Haglund in the Colonial Revival style. Colonial Revival homes typically are rectangular, two to three stories, with gable roofs, simple classical detailing and symmetrical façades, with wood or brick siding and multi-pane, double-hung windows with shutters. Colonial Revival architecture was a popular American house style from the 1870s to the 1950s.

Little is known about the Larkin home's original owners, N.A. Humbaugh and his wife, Audrey, who resided there a short while. In 1943, Henry H. and Edith McKinnies purchased it and lived there with their only child, Henry Jr., who was later to become Jeffrey Hunter.

Hunter attended Whitefish Bay schools. He was a member of the high school student council (and its president his senior year), the dramatic club and the "Hi-Y" club. He also lettered in football and was co-captain his senior year. He played leading roles in high school plays, acted in productions of the North Shore Children's Theater and performed in summer stock with future Oscar winners Eileen Heckart and Morton DaCosta and Tony winner Charlotte Rae. He also was a radio actor at WTMJ, getting his first acting paycheck in 1945 for the wartime series *Those Who Serve.*

After high school, McKinnies enlisted in the U.S. Navy, serving for one year before receiving a medical discharge. He then attended Northwestern University, graduated with a bachelor's degree in 1949 and further honed

Picture of Hunter as Jesus in *King of Kings*, 1961, released on Blu-ray in 2011. *MGM promotional photograph.*

his acting skills. He studied under Alvina Krauss, who also taught such Hollywood luminaries as Charlton Heston, Tony Randall, Cloris Leachman, Claude Akins, Jerry Orbach, Ann-Margret and Warren Beatty. Years later, she stated that Hunter was the most talented student she ever had.

Hunter was working on his master's degree at UCLA when he was discovered during a school production and in 1950 shot his first film for 20th Century Fox. Studio head Darryl F. Zanuck changed his name to Jeffrey Hunter. Within two years, Hunter had worked his way to top billing in *Sailor of the King* (1953). His big break came in *The Searchers* (1956) with John Wayne, and in 1960 Hunter had one of his best roles in *Hell to Eternity* (1960). That year, Hunter landed the role for which he is probably best known (although it's considered far from his best work) as Jesus in *King of Kings*. He made thirty-five films during his twenty-year career.

After starring for two years in a TV western series, *Temple Houston*, Hunter made a momentous career decision. Cast as the captain of the USS *Enterprise* in *Star Trek* in 1964, Hunter quit the role after shooting the pilot episode, deciding to concentrate on his movie career. Footage from the pilot was later incorporated into a two-part episode in *Star Trek*'s first season, but the producers were forced to recast Hunter for a new actor and captain, James Kirk, played by William Shatner.

Hunter later lobbied to be cast as Mike Brady for the TV series *The Brady Bunch* (1969), but the producer would not consider him, telling Hunter he was "too good-looking to be an architect."

Hunter died in 1969 after a series of medical misfortunes almost as dramatic as his acting roles. Hunter was injured in an on-set explosion while shooting a film in Spain, suffering facial lacerations from broken glass and powder burns. Later, he was accidentally hit on the chin with a karate chop when he failed to defend himself in time, banging his head against a door. Then, while on the plane returning to the United States, he suffered a stroke. Hunter recovered and, shortly after signing to star in *The Desperados* (1969), suffered another stroke while on stairs in his home, fracturing his skull in the fall. He died on May 27 without regaining consciousness at age forty-two.

JANE ARCHER

Actress Jane Archer. *Promotional photograph.*

Jane Archer was born in Connecticut in 1910. In the early 1930s, she went to Vienna, Austria, to attend the Max Reinhardt School of Acting. Among the instructors at the Reinhardt School of Acting was Otto Preminger, who eventually became a famous director and actor in the United States. While at the school, Archer helped Preminger learn English.[84] While attending this school, Archer met Horst Schillbach, an engineering student at the University of Munich.

After returning to the United States, Archer acted on the Broadway stage for four years with Helen Hayes, Ruth Gordon, Robert Sherwood, Alfred Lunt and Lynne Fontanne. Among her acting credits, she stared in *Libel*, directed by Otto Preminger.

Archer continued to correspond with Schillbach, who traveled to the United States and considered a number of job offers. He decided, however, to return to Germany and encouraged Archer to join him.

In August 1938, armed with a letter of recommendation from Lynne Fontanne, Archer took a position with the English Repertory Theater in Berlin, under what was supposed to be a one-year contract.

Archer and Schillbach married a month later, shortly before the war broke out. Once the war started, it was difficult for the couple to move. Schillbach was employed as a research engineer at the Siemens electronics plant in Berlin. Archer continued to act with the English Repertory Theater, performing in *The Millionairess*, *Mary Stewart*, *George and Margaret*, *French Without Tears* and other well-known works and classics.

Archer continued to perform in the theater until 1944, when eventually all of the young male actors were drafted into the armed forces. She attempted to leave Berlin but eventually returned to be with her husband. In 1945, with the outcome of the war obvious, Archer and her husband left Berlin and headed to the west as Russian troops began storming into Germany.

After the war, the couple worked with the United Nations Recovery and Rehabilitation group. The two eventually made their way to the United States—Archer in 1946 and Schillbach shortly afterward. Archer traveled across the country for a time on lecture tours, but in 1948 the couple moved to 5251 North Idlewild Avenue in Whitefish Bay. They had one son, Robert, born in 1949.

In the 1960s, Archer performed a one-person show entitled *Helen Hayes: Life-Career-Roles* in which she tells details from Hayes' life and dramatizes scenes from several plays.[85] She also developed a program for women's and other club functions, specializing in dramatic readings.[86]

Archer died on March 28, 1999, at the age of eighty-nine; her husband, Dr. Horst Martin Schillbach, died on December 8, 2002, at the age of ninety-four. Dr. Schillbach is believed to have lived in the Whitefish Bay residence until at least the year 2000.

In 2012, a book that Jane Archer wrote about her experience during the war in Germany was published, entitled *Enemy Bride, Life and Survival in Nazi Rule*. She wrote the book over a lengthy period, believed to have been between 1949 and the early 1960s. The transcripts were edited by Annabel Ascher.

KRISTEN JOHNSTON

Actress Kristen Johnston. *Promotional photograph.*

Actress Kristen Johnston lived in Whitefish Bay with her mother, Angela Johnston, during her high school years. Kristen's father was Rod Johnson, a Wisconsin state senator. Her mother was a real estate agent.

Kristen is best known for her role portraying Sally Solomon in the TV series *3rd Rock from the Sun* (also known as *Life as We Know It* and *3rd Rock*), which ran on the NBC network (1996–2001). However, she has had numerous other theatrical roles.[87]

Kristen attended St. Eugene's Catholic Grade School before starting at Whitefish Bay High School, where she graduated in 1985. While in Whitefish Bay, Kristen lived at 4716 North Wilshire Road. She went on to college at New York University and earned a bachelor's of fine arts degree in drama.

Kristen Johnston was involved in the American Field Service program while in high school, and she spent some of her teen years as an exchange student in Sweden and in South America. AFS is an international, not-for-profit organization that each year provides hundreds of American high school students the opportunity to live and study in a foreign land.

For her portrayal of Sally Solomon on *3rd Rock from the Sun*, Kristen received an Emmy Award in 1997 and was nominated for Best Supporting Actress in a Comedy Series in 1998. Kristen also received nominations for Golden Globe, Screen Actors Guild and the American Comedy Award.

JULIUS PETER HEIL

Julius Peter Heil was born in Dussmund-an-der-Mosel, Germany, in 1876. He immigrated as a child to the United States when he was five.

At age fourteen, Heil started work at the Milwaukee Harvester Company as a drill-press operator. He later took a job with the Falk Corporation, where he worked installing welded steel track for street railways throughout South America.

When he turned twenty-five, Heil started up his own company to weld railway tracks—it was called the Heil Rail Joint Welding Company. As other product lines were introduced, the name was shortened to the Heil Co. The company eventually grew into a major manufacturing concern, producing road machinery, tanks for storage and transportation, dump-truck bodies and furnaces for home heating.

In the 1930s, Heil began to get involved in politics. He was appointed in 1933 to lead the Wisconsin advisory board for the National Recovery Administration—a New Deal agency of Franklin D. Roosevelt to bring industry, labor and government together to create "fair practices."

A Republican, Julius Heil ran a successful campaign for governor of Wisconsin in 1938, defeating Philip F. La Follette. He was elected to a second term two years later. During his administration, he reorganized the tax and welfare departments, modernized the state's accounting practices and established a state department of securities. He also helped to enact the Wisconsin employment peace act, regarded as a precursor to the federal Taft-Hartley Act.

Julius Peter Heil. *Wikipedia Commons.*

While governor, he toured the country promoting Wisconsin's dairy industry. He was known as "Julius the Just." The *New York Times* reported that Heil was also known for clowning and silly antics.[88]

Heil was defeated in his attempt for a third term and returned to his business, serving as chairman of the board of the Heil Company until his death in 1949.

TOM MILLER (PRODUCER/WRITER OF THE *HAPPY DAYS* TV SHOW)

Thomas Lee "Tom" Miller was born on August 31, 1940, and lived with his parents at 6017 North Bay Ridge Avenue in Whitefish Bay. He started his career as a development executive at Paramount and 20th Century Fox and eventually became assistant director to Billy Wilder. He was writer of *The Year of the Horse* in 1966, and in 1969, he was placed in charge of development for *The Immortal.* He performed the same job in the 1970s for *Weekend of Terror* and *Assault on the Wayne.*

He formed his own production company in 1970, with Edward K. Milkis, as Miller-Milkis Productions. A year after starting the company, he co-created *Nanny and the Professor* with the late A.J. Carothers. He wrote episodes for *Nanny and the Professor* and *Me and the Chimp* and co-created that show with Garry Marshall. Miller co-produced the feature films *Silver Streak* (1976) and *Foul Play* (1978) with Edward Milkis.

Tom Miller is perhaps known best for his TV sitcoms and locally known as the producer of *Happy Days*—one of ABC's longest-running sitcoms. It aired from January 15, 1974, to July 12, 1984, and the reruns continue to live on in syndication. Approximately 255 episodes were made, which must have astounded Paramount and ABC, who initially thought the show was likely to go off the air after only thirteen weeks. The show was the number one rated TV show in America during the 1976–77 season with a 31.5 rating—spin-off *Laverne & Shirley* finished second with a 30.9 rating.

Happy Days began as a pilot in 1971 called "New Family in Town," which was produced by Garry Marshall for ABC. The pilot contained some of the same characters (Richie, Howard, Marion and Potsie) and some of the same actors (Ron Howard, Marion Ross and Anson Williams).

The city of Milwaukee was chosen as the location in which Happy Days was set. The producers felt that Milwaukee gave the show a Midwest flavor that would appeal to a broad audience.

The show had two main sets: the Cunningham home and Arnold's Drive-In. The Milky Way Drive-In, located on Port Washington Road in the North Shore suburb of Glendale, Wisconsin, now Kopp's Frozen Custard Stand, was reportedly the inspiration for the original Arnold's Drive-In. College pennants adorned the walls, including Purdue and the University of Wisconsin–Milwaukee, along with a blue and white sign reading, "Jefferson High School." Milwaukee's Washington High School provided the inspiration for the exteriors of the fictional Jefferson High. Milwaukee Braves home-run king Hank Aaron appeared in one episode.

Kopp's Drive-In, taken in 1959, when Tom Miller lived in Whitefish Bay. *Whitefish Bay Historical Society.*

A current view of Kopp's Drive-In, taken in August 2013. *Whitefish Bay Historical Society.*

There were several spinoffs of *Happy Days*:

- *Laverne & Shirley* featuring Laverne DeFazio (Penny Marshall) and Shirley Feeney (Cindy Williams), who both appeared in a 1975 *Happy Days* episode.
- *Mork and Mindy* featuring Robin Williams' space alien character, Mork from Ork. Robin Williams appeared on *Happy Days* in February 1978.
- *Joanie Loves Chachi* with Erin Moran and Scott Baio.
- A Saturday morning animated version called *The Fonz and the Happy Days Gang* aired from November 1980 to November 1981.

As a producer, Tom Miller was involved in thirty-one titles, most of which were TV sitcoms. He is also listed as writer for nine titles and had several other movie development roles.[89] Many of his sitcoms were based in the Midwest. In addition to *Laverne & Shirley* and *Happy Days*, *Step by Step* was set in nearby Port Washington. *Family Matters*, *Perfect Strangers* and *Two of a Kind* were all set in Chicago.

HERMAN A. UIHLEIN

We all know where the Uihlein "mansion" is located in Whitefish Bay and know that the Uihleins were involved in some way with the Schlitz Brewing Co. But who was Herman A. Uihlein?

Herman Uihlein was born in 1886 as the son of longtime Joseph Schlitz Brewing Company president Henry Uihlein. While he was heir to a substantial family fortune, Herman was not closely involved with the daily operation of the brewery—although he did serve on its board. He graduated from Cornell University in 1908, studied law at Columbia for two years and took his first job in 1911, when he was appointed president of the newly formed Lavine Gear Company, a manufacturer of steering gears for trucks.

Herman and Claudia Uihlein's residence was the first constructed in the "Pabst Whitefish Bay subdivision." It was built on the former grounds of one of Wisconsin's great beer gardens, the Pabst Whitefish Bay Resort. In 1915, the Uihlein family purchased a lot near where the bandstand stood. Although suburban homes had already begun to dot the landscape, replacing farmland and changing the character of the old fishing village, the Uihlein house introduced a new scale to the village. Completed after three years of work, the house was larger and more pretentious than any earlier, or later, house in Whitefish Bay.

Above: Herman Uihlein and his wife, Claudia, with their large family. *Whitefish Bay Historical Society.*

Right: This interesting view of the front entrance to the Herman and Claudia Uihlein home shows the wrought-iron grill incorporated into the front doorway, designed by master craftsman Cyril Colnik. *Whitefish Bay Historical Society.*

Together with his wife, the former Claudia Holt, Herman Uihlein was a leading patron of the Milwaukee Philharmonic symphony orchestra.

Uihlein served as president of Lavine Gear (which later became known as the Ben-Hur Manufacturing Company) until his death in 1942 at the age of fifty-two. After his death, Mrs. Uihlein remained at the house until 1946, when it was sold to a real estate holding company.

PETER AND JENNIFER (HEIL) BUFFETT

Peter Andrew Buffett is the son of Omaha billionaire Warren E. Buffett, who controls Berkshire Hathaway, Inc., a diversified holding company. Peter is a music composer, musician and producer.

Peter was born in 1958 in Omaha, Nebraska—the second son of Warren and Susan Buffett. He graduated from Central High School in Omaha and attended Stanford University.

He began his musical career in San Francisco, producing albums for local musicians. He also was hired to write commercials for various clients, including Coca-Cola, MTV and CNN.

Eventually, he came to the attention of Milwaukee-based producer Narada Productions, which signed him to a recording contract. Shortly after his first Narada album was released,[90] Buffet moved to Milwaukee and purchased the Uihlein manson. He met Jennifer Heil at a local restaurant in 1991; they were married in 1996.

Jennifer Heil was born in 1966, along with her twin brother, Joseph Lewis. They both attended and graduated from Whitefish Bay's Dominican High School.[91] Jennifer put herself through college at Cardinal Stritch University and worked for a company that published city guides.

After the couple married, Warren Buffett gave them $100,000 and specified that it be used for charity. Peter and Jennifer established a foundation to help distribute the money. In 2006, Warren Buffett announced that he was giving their foundation $1 billion in Berkshire Hathaway stock.

Peter and Jennifer's NoVo Foundation (the name comes from the Latin word for "to create") is focused on creating a more just and balanced world based on cooperation and partnership, primarily through the empowerment of girls and women. NoVo works to achieve its vision by investing in strategic initiatives that have the potential to lead to systemic change, specifically ending violence against girls and women, unlocking

Peter and Jennifer (Heil) Buffett surrounded by children during one of their visits to Africa on behalf of the NoVo Foundation.

the potential of adolescent girls and advancing whole child education and social and emotional learning. To allow Peter time for his music business, Jennifer acts as the fund's main administrator.

Peter and Jennifer Buffett lived in Whitefish Bay until 2004, when they sold the Uihlein residence and moved to New York. Peter later referred to the purchase of the Whitefish Bay mansion as his "big house blunder."[92] Buffett explained that his relocation to Whitefish Bay and purchase of the "big house" settled him with hefty house payments, caused him to have to travel much more and kept him from doing more of what he really wanted to do.

The couple visits the Milwaukee area frequently to see family and friends.

NOTES

CHAPTER 2

1. Threshing is the process used to separate the chaff, the protective covering around the grain and the grain from a plant's stalk. During the nineteenth century, farmers used a variety of methods to remove the chaff and grain from the stalk and to crack open the chaff. Some used flails and others, animal-powered machines. Today, farmers primarily thresh with gasoline-powered machines.

CHAPTER 5

2. The terms "pound net" and "pond Net" have both been used to describe the fishing process employed. The later term may be more correct.

CHAPTER 6

3. An artesian well is one drilled through impermeable strata to reach water capable of rising to the surface by internal hydrostatic pressure. It freely flows without pumping. This artesian well may have given Silver Spring Drive its name.

Chapter 7

4. Corner of Henry Clay and Woodruff.

Chapter 8

5. This article appears to have been written by Mimi Bird for publication in a local newspaper.
6. The Anna McGee who relayed the events to Mimi Bird was Charles' wife.

Chapter 11

7. This story was written by Gloria Rockwood Houghton in the year 2000. It is included by the permission of her family. A version of this story was also published in the *Orlando Sentinel* on June 3, 2000.

Chapter 16

8. *Milwaukee Journal*, "Tompkins Principal in Village Zone War," Sunday, December 9, 1923, part 1, 10.
9. Dennis McCann, "Echoes of a Murder Long Ago," *Milwaukee Journal Magazine*, Sunday, July 11, 1993, 5.
10. *Milwaukee Journal*, "Tompkins Bit Queer Since Early Life, Alienists Find," Monday, December 17, 1923, part 1, 2.
11. 1900 U.S. Census "occupation" listing for Edward Ray Tompkins on farm property of Samuel A. Tompkins.
12. *Milwaukee Journal*, "It's Done, Why Cry? Asks Wife Murderer," Sunday, December 9, 1923, part 1, 1.
13. *Milwaukee Journal*, "Love Letters Show Romance That Culminated in Tragedy," Sunday, December 9, part 1, 11.
14. *Weekly Clintonian*, "Miss Ora Clover Becomes Bride of E.R. Tompkins," September 9, 1910, 1.
15. Now 3210 North Marietta Avenue.
16. *Milwaukee Journal*, "It's Done, Why Cry?"
17. *Milwaukee Journal*, "Scrapbook Bares Why of Wife's Martyrdom," Wednesday, December 19, 1923, part 1, 2.
18. *Milwaukee Journal*, "Will C. Conrad Dies; At *Journal* 45 Years," November 27, 1970, part 2, 1.

19. These addresses are now, respectively, 2860 North Cramer Street and 2969 North Murray Avenue.
20. A phrase often used by Ora to describe Ray's efforts, quoted in a letter written by my great-grandmother Mary Tompkins to a niece named Maud Young, mailed on January 1, 1924. The letter was given to my mother, who passed it on in her memorabilia.
21. *Milwaukee Journal*, "Heart Steeled, Dad Sees Son; Has No Sympathy for 'Best Son a Father Ever Had,'" Sunday, December 9, 1923, part 1, 1, 11.
22. Those addresses, respectively, are now 2525 East Stratford Court and 2503 East Stratford Court.
23. John M. Barry, *The Great Influenza: The Epic Story of the Deadliest Plague in History* (New York: Viking Press [Penguin Group], 2004).
24. H. Russell Austin, *The Milwaukee Story: The Making of an American City* (Milwaukee, WI: Journal Company, 1946), 81.
25. Eileen A. Lynch, "It Started with a Cough in the Summer of 1918," *Pennsylvania Gazette*, October 28, 1998.
26. Barry, *Great Influenza*, 397.
27. Harry R. Zander, "Slayer First Sees Real Wife in Lines of Diary," *Milwaukee Journal*, Tuesday, December 11, 1923, part 1, 1.
28. Ibid.
29. *Milwaukee Journal*, "The Victim's Diary," Monday, December 10, 1923, part 1, 1–2.
30. *Milwaukee Journal*, "Two Small Children Are Real Victims of Tragedy," Saturday, December 8, 1923, part 1, 1.
31. *Milwaukee Journal*, "Inspiration Girl Picked by Geometry, Say Files," Thursday, December 13, 1923, part 1, 1.
32. Ibid.
33. That address is now 1624 West Mineral Street.
34. *Milwaukee Journal*, "Girl Calm, Sure, in Giving Denial; Miss Witmeyer is Emphatic in Refutation of Charges," Thursday, December 13, 1923, part 1, 2.
35. Ibid.
36. *Milwaukee Journal*, "Slayer Planned to Wed Girl, Letters Show; Pre-Nuptial Agreement Drawn Up to Cover Tompkins' Estate and Religion of Children," Saturday, December 15, 1923, part 1, 1–2.
37. *Milwaukee Journal*, "Inspiration Girl."
38. *Milwaukee Journal*, "Slayer Planned to Wed Girl."
39. Zander, "Slayer First Sees Real Wife."
40. *Milwaukee Journal*, "Witmeyer Girl Faces Charges; Bail Set in District Court Hearing: Tells of Illicit Love," Monday, December 10, 1923, part 1, 1.

41. *Milwaukee Journal*, "Relatives Deny Girl Was a Dupe; Tompkins' Kin Declare Miss Witmeyer's Story Will Not Hold," Friday, December 14, 1923, part 1, 2.
42. *Milwaukee Journal*, "Girl Calm, Sure."
43. *Milwaukee Journal*, "Girl Pours Out Praise in Letters to Tompkins," Tuesday, December 11, 1923, part 1, 17.
44. *Milwaukee Journal*, "The Victim's Diary."
45. *Milwaukee Journal*, "Tompkins Bit Queer."
46. *Milwaukee Journal*, "Orders Probe of Tompkins' Release From Hospital; Doctor Asserts Advice to Hold Was Rejected: Man Insane, His Warning, but Was Freed; Petition for Incarceration Lost," Tuesday, December 11, 1923, part 1, 1.
47. *Milwaukee Journal*, "Probe Release of Mad Man by Hospital; Shaughnessy Takes Testimony on Freeing of Tompkins after Doctor Held Him Insane," Wednesday, December 12, 1923, part 1, 1–2.
48. *Milwaukee Journal*, "Asks Prison Sentence for Slayer's Sweetheart; Doctor Blamed in Hospital Quiz; Mueller Called Again After Miss Getts Holds Man Responsible," Friday, December 14, 1923, part 1, 1–2.
49. *Milwaukee Journal*, "Probe Release of Mad Man."
50. *Milwaukee Journal*, "Girl Calm, Sure."
51. Ibid.
52. *Milwaukee Journal*, "Normal School 'Fired' Slayer; Dismissal Followed Charges of Intimacy with Teacher," Sunday, December 9, 1923, part 1, 10.
53. *Milwaukee Journal*, "Killer's Letters to Wife Reveal Turmoil in Brain," Thursday, December 13, 1923, part 1, 14.
54. *Milwaukee Journal*, "Girl Calm, Sure."
55. *Milwaukee Journal*, "Relatives Deny Girl Was a Dupe."
56. *Milwaukee Journal*, "Letter Key to Murder," Sunday, December 9, 1923, part 1, 1.
57. Zander, "Slayer First Sees Real Wife."
58. *Sunday Sentinel*, "Daughter, 10 Years Old, Tells of Terror Reign of Tompkins," December 9, 1923, part 1, 10.
59. *Evening Sentinel*, "Girl's Phone Call Started Death Search," Saturday, December 8, 1923, part 1, 1.
60. *Milwaukee Journal*, "Confesses Murder of His Wife; Chokes Victim, Cuts Off Head," Saturday, December 8, 1923, part 1, 1.
61. Russell Baker, *The Good Times* (New York: The Penguin Group, 1989), 76.
62. Zander, "Slayer First Sees Real Wife."
63. *Milwaukee Sentinel*, "Hundreds Attracted to Scene of Tragedy," Monday, December 10, 1923, part 1, 4.

64. *Milwaukee Journal*, "4,000 Visit Morgue," Monday, December 10, 1923, part 1, 2.
65. *Milwaukee Journal*, "Asks Prison Sentence," 1–2.
66. *Milwaukee Sentinel*, "Five Alienists to Examine Tompkins; Commission's Verdict Will Determine Charge Against Slayer," Wednesday, December 12, 1923, part 1, 6.
67. *Milwaukee Sentinel*, "Tompkins Case Frightens Wives; Score of Women Besiege Prosecutor for 'Protection' From Husbands," December 11, 1923, part 1, 1.
68. *Milwaukee Journal*, "Five Alienists to Test Slayer; Second Appearance in Court Brief as First; Court Enters Plea," Tuesday, December 11, 1923, part 1, 1–2.
69. *Milwaukee Journal*, "Slayer of Wife Sees Children; Youngsters Permitted to See Father Before Going to Indiana," Wednesday, December 19, 1923, part 1, 2.
70. *Milwaukee Journal*, "Crowd Disappointed," Thursday, December 20, 1923, part 1, 1.
71. *Milwaukee Journal*, "Slayer Enters Portals Where Exit Is Unused; Likely to Remain in Asylum Long Time, Doctor Says; Jovial on Auto Trip," Thursday, December 20, 1923, part 1, 1, 11.

CHAPTER 17

72. According to Wikipedia, the term "blind pig" originated in the United States in the nineteenth century; it was applied to lower-class establishments that sold alcoholic beverages illegally. The operator of an establishment (such as a saloon or bar) would charge customers to see an attraction (such as an animal) and then serve a "complimentary" alcoholic beverage, thus circumventing the law.

CHAPTER 19

73. Included with the permission of the family of Gloria Rockwood Houghton.

CHAPTER 21

74. There was at least one other Grams family living in the area at the time, that being the family of Christopher and Henrietta Grams and Christopher's father, Johann.
75. "A Long Fish Story and Lots of Fish: From 1862 to 1921," recollections of Mary Jane Scheife, Mimi Bird files, Whitefish Bay Library. Pound net fishing is also commonly referred to as pond net fishing.

CHAPTER 22

76. Howard Conrad, ed., *History of Milwaukee County: From Its First Settlement to the Year 1895,* Vol. 2, 356.
77. A "proprietary business" is one that possesses private ownership with exclusive rights of use protected by copyright, patent or trademark. In this case, it refers to a company that produced over-the-counter drugs and nutritional supplements.
78. Most of the above information was taken from a bio in a history of Milwaukee County. Morrison was about thirty when it was written.
79. From the *Pneumatic*, described as a "progressive monthly publication for cyclists, published in Milwaukee in 1892. This quote is from the June 15, 1892 issue (page 4).
80. This home is also known as the "Suburban Club" and W.H. Goodall's Building.
81. As reported in *American Bookmaker: A Journal of Technical Art and Information* (August 1890).
82. "A. Cressy Morrison," *Chemical and Engineering News* 20, no. 12 (June 23, 1942).
83. Hans Albrecht Bethe was a German American nuclear physicist and Nobel laureate in physics for his work on the theory of stellar nucleosynthesis. A versatile theoretical physicist, Bethe also made important contributions to quantum electrodynamics, nuclear physics, solid-state physics and astrophysics. During World War II, he was head of the Theoretical Division at the secret Los Alamos laboratory where the atomic bomb was first developed. While there, he played a key role in calculating the critical mass of the weapons and did theoretical work on the implosion method used in both the Trinity test and the "Fat Man" weapon dropped on Nagasaki, Japan. For most of his career, Bethe was a professor at Cornell University.

84. Most of the information on Jane Archer and Horst Schillbach was obtained from *Milwaukee Journal* articles, including an interview with Jane Archer in which the actress recalled her wartime experiences, entitled "Actress Recalls Years in Nazi Germany During War," by Steve Maersch. She was also interviewed for a July 17, 1997 article in the *Milwaukee Journal-Sentinel* entitled "A Survivor, Jane Archer Schillbach Has Quite a Story to Tell."
85. *Milwaukee Journal*, "Theater: They Dare to Act Solo," June 6, 1962.
86. *St. Petersburg Times*, "Actress to Perform at Club Dinner," November 26, 1976.
87. Including her portrayal of Ivana Humpalot in the Austin Powers film *The Spy Who Shagged Me.*
88. *New York Times*, "Heil's Antics Jolt Wisconsin," June 4, 1939, E10.
89. Based on website IMDb's listing of Tom Miller's film career.
90. Peter Buffett's first Narada album was entitled *The Waiting.* He had his first major success while at Narada, scoring the "Fire Dance" scene in the film *Dances with Wolves.* The film score, which was composed by John Barry, won an Academy Award. Among his many album titles is the soundtrack for *Wisconsin: An American Portrait.*
91. Additional Whitefish Bay connections: Jennifer's father, Joseph Heil Sr., may have lived in Whitefish Bay for a time, as did her twin brother, Joseph Heil Jr. Jennifer's mother, Barbara, taught for a time at Dominican High School. It is unknown whether Jennifer Heil is related to Julius Heil, former governor of Wisconsin, who is also featured in this chapter.
92. Peter Buffett, *Life Is What You Make It: Find Your Own Path to Fulfillment* (New York: Three Rivers Press, 2011).

INDEX

U

W

ABOUT THE AUTHOR

I am an engineer by training and practice, having worked for over forty years at "keeping the lights on." My wife, Suzan, and I have lived in the village since 1973, during which time we have raised three kids, paid our taxes and enjoyed living among our neighbors.

I've come to think of myself as a fisherman of history, casting a net for information about the community's early history. This fascination with history occurred almost by accident. I didn't really enjoy history in school because of the rote memorization of events and dates that seemed to be required. But early in my career, I had a boss who encouraged me to give back to my profession by volunteering. Taking to the call, I attended a local meeting of the American Society of Mechanical Engineers (ASME) and offered my services. Never a group to turn away free help, they assigned me to an open position as chair of the History and Heritage Committee. I found the assignment to be very rewarding. Thirty-five years later, industrial archaeology continues to be an important part of my life.

My foray into history continued after my retirement, when I was appointed to the village's Historic Preservation Commission. During this time, I started to explore Whitefish Bay history and discovered that I truly enjoy "fishing" for historical information. For me, these stories illustrate that when you cast your bait into the waters of the village's history, you truly never know what you're going to find at the end of the line!

It has given me great pleasure to explore Whitefish Bay's amazing history, and I am grateful for the chance to share it with you all—just don't ask me to keep track of the dates!

www.ingramcontent.com/pod-product-compliance
Lightning Source LLC
LaVergne TN
LVHW010943100826
845153LV00002B/131

* 9 7 8 1 5 4 0 2 2 2 3 7 4 *